Books by Margaret Poynter

GOLD RUSH! The Yukon Stampede of 1898
SEARCH & RESCUE: The Team and the Missions
VOYAGER: The Story of a Space Mission (*with Arthur L. Lane*)
TOO FEW HAPPY ENDINGS: The Dilemma of the Humane
    Societies
WILDLAND FIRE FIGHTING
UNDER THE HIGH SEAS: New Frontiers in Oceanography
    (*with Donald Collins*)
COSMIC QUEST: Searching for Intelligent Life Among the Stars
    (*with Michael J. Klein*)

Cosmic Quest

Cosmic Quest

Searching for Intelligent Life Among the Stars

*by Margaret Poynter
and Michael J. Klein*

ILLUSTRATED WITH PHOTOGRAPHS AND DIAGRAMS

*Atheneum • New York
1984*

Title page photograph of the spiral galaxy in Andromeda courtesy of Mount Palomar Observatory

Library of Congress Cataloging in Publication Data
Poynter, Margaret.   Cosmic quest.

  Bibliography: p. 117
  Includes index.
  Summary: Describes the work of the SETI (Search for Extraterrestrial Intelligence) Project, founded by an international group of scientists committed to finding some signs of intelligent life beyond the Earth.
   1. Life on other planets—Juvenile literature.
  2. Interstellar communication—Juvenile literature.
  [1. Life on other planets. 2. Interstellar communication]
  I. Klein, Michael J., 1940 Jan. 19– . II. Title.
  QB54.P68   1984   574.999   84-6191
  ISBN 0-689-31068-4

Copyright © 1984 by Margaret Poynter and Michael J. Klein
All rights reserved
Published simultaneously in Canada by
McClelland & Stewart, Ltd.
Composition by Dix Type Inc., Syracuse, New York
Printed and bound by Fairfield Graphics, Fairfield, Pennsylvania
Designed by Mary Ahern
First Edition

To our parents,

our link with the past

To our children,

our hope for the future

Acknowledgments

To Bob for answering endless questions.

To Barbara for encouraging one of us (MJK) to put some ideas in print.

To the students in our local schools for asking those tough, thoughtful questions.

Our thanks go to Don DeVincenzi, Robert C. Edgar and Samuel Gulkis for reading the manuscript and offering constructive comments and valuable suggestions.

JPL Engineer James Withington and SETI Scientist Edward T. Olsen were patient and willing photographic subjects.

The International SETI Petition

The International SETI petition is printed here with an up-to-date list of signatories. The petition was prepared by Carl Sagan, with Planetary Society logistical support, and organized by Mary Maki.

THE HUMAN SPECIES is now able to communicate with other civilizations in space, if such exist. Using current radioastronomical technology, it is possible for us to receive signals from civilizations no more advanced than we are over a distance of at least many thousands of light years. The cost of a systematic international research effort, using existing radiotelescopes, is as low as a few million dollars per year for one or two decades. The program would be more than a million times more thorough than all previous searches, by all nations, put together. The results—whether positive or negative—would have profound implications for our view of our universe and ourselves.

WE BELIEVE such a coordinated search program is well-justified on its scientific merits. It will also have important subsidiary benefits for radioastronomy in general. It is a scientific activity that seems likely to garner substantial public support. In addition, because of the growing problem of radiofrequency interference by civilian and military transmitters, the search program will become more difficult the longer we wait. This is the time to begin.

IT HAS BEEN SUGGESTED that the apparent absence of a major reworking of the Galaxy by very advanced beings, or the apparent absence of extraterrestrial colonists in the solar system demonstrates that there are no extraterrestrial intelligent beings anywhere. At the very least, this argument depends on a major extrapolation from the circumstances on Earth, here and now. The radio search, on the other hand, assumes nothing about other civilizations that has not transpired in ours.

THE UNDERSIGNED are scientists from a variety of disciplines and nations who have considered the problem of extraterrestrial intelligence —some of us for more than 20 years. We represent a wide variety of opinion on the abundance of extraterrestrials, on the ease of establishing contact, and on the validity of arguments of the sort summarized in the first sentence of the previous paragraph. But we are unanimous in our conviction that the only significant test of the existence of extraterrestrial intelligence is an experimental one. No *a priori* arguments on this subject can be compelling or should be used as a substitute for an observational program. We urge the organization of a coordinated, worldwide and systematic search for extraterrestrial intelligence.

Sagan, Carl, David Duncan Professor of Astronomy and Space Sciences; Director, Laboratory for Planetary Studies, Center for Radiophysics and Space Research, Cornell University.
Baltimore, David, Director, Whitehead Institute for Biomedical Research and Professor of Biology, Massachusetts Institute of Technology, Nobel Laureate in Physiology and Medicine
Berendzen, Richard, President, American University
Billingham, John, Chief Extraterrestrial Research Division, NASA Ames Research Center
Burbidge, E. Margaret, Professor of Astronomy and Director, Center for Astrophysics and Space Sciences, University of California, San Diego; Former Director, Royal Greenwich Observatory, U.K.; President, American Association for the Advancement of Science; Past President, American Astronomical Society
Calvin, Melvin, University Professor of Chemistry and Former Director, Laboratory of Chemical Biodynamics, University of California at Berkeley, Nobel Laureate in Chemistry
Cameron, A. G. W., Professor of Astronomy, Harvard University; Former Chairman, Space Science Board, National Research Council/ National Academy of Sciences
Chadha, M. S., Senior Researcher, Bhabha Atomic Research Centre, Bombay, India
Chandrasekhar, S., Morton D. Hull Distinguished Service Professor of Physics and Astrophysics, University of Chicago; National Medal of Science
Crick, Francis, Distinguished Research Professor, Salk Institute; Nobel Laureate in Physiology and Medicine
Dixon, Robert S., Assistant Director, Ohio State University Radio Observatory
Donahue, T. M., Professor of Atmospheric Sciences, University of Michigan; Chairman, Space Science Board, National Research Council/National Academy of Sciences
Drake, Frank D., Goldwin Smith Professor of Astronomy, Cornell University; Former Director, National Astronomy and Ionosphere Center
DuBridge, Lee A., President Emeritus, California Institute of Technology; Former Presidential Science Advisor
Dyson, Freeman J., Professor of Physics, Institute for Advanced Study, Princeton
Eigen, Manfred, Director, Section on Biochemical Kinetics, Max Planck Institute for Biophysical Chemistry, Göttingen, German Federal Republic, Nobel Laureate in Chemistry
Eisner, Thomas, Jacob Gould Schurman Professor of Biology, Cornell University
Elliot, James L., Associate Professor of Astronomy and Physics and Director, George R. Wallace Jr. Astrophysical Observatory, Massachusetts Institute of Technology

Field, George B., Senior Scientist, Smithsonian Astrophysical Observatory, and Professor of Astronomy, Harvard University; Former Director of the Harvard-Smithsonian Center for Astrophysics
Ginzburg, Vitaly L., Senior Staff Member, Lebedev Physical Institute, Moscow; Lenin Prize Laureate
Gold, Thomas, John L. Wetherill Professor of Astronomy and Former Director, Center for Radiophysics and Space Research, Cornell University
Goldberg, Leo, Former Director, Kitt Peak National Observatory; Past President, International Astronomical Union
Goldreich, Peter, Lee A. DuBridge Professor of Astrophysics and Planetary Physics, California Institute of Technology
Gott, J. Richard, III, Associate Professor of Astrophysics, Princeton University
Gould, Stephen Jay, Professor of Geology, and Alexander Agassiz Professor of Zoology, Harvard University
Hagfors, Tor, Director, National Astronomy and Ionosphere Center, Professor of Electrical Engineering, Cornell University; Former Professor of Electrical Engineering, University of Trondheim, Norway
Hawking, Stephen W., Lucasian Professor of Mathematics, Cambridge University, U.K.
Heeschen, David S., Senior Scientist and Former Director, National Radio Astronomy Observatory
Heidmann, Jean, Chief Astronomer, Paris Observatory
Herzberg, Gerhard, Distinguished Research Scientist, National Research Council of Canada; Nobel Laureate in Chemistry
Hesburgh, Rev. Theodore, President, University of Notre Dame
Horowitz, Paul, Professor of Physics, Harvard University
Hoyle, Fred, Former Plumian Professor of Astronomy and Experimental Philosophy and Former Director of the Institute of Astronomy, Cambridge University, U.K.
Jones, Eric M., Staff Member, Los Alamos Scientific Laboratory
Jugaku, Jun, Professor of Astronomy, University of Tokyo, Japan
Kardashev, N. S., Director, Samarkand Radio Observatory, Institute for Cosmic Research, Soviet Academy of Sciences, Moscow
Kellermann, Kenneth I., Senior Scientist, National Radio Astronomy Observatory
Klein, Michael J., Senior Scientist, Jet Propulsion Laboratory, NASA
Lee, Richard B., Professor of Anthropology, University of Toronto, Canada
Lindblad, Per-Olof, Professor of Astronomy and Director of the Stockholm Observatory, Stockholm, Sweden
MacLean, Paul D., Chief, Laboratory of Brain Evolution and Behavior, National Institute of Mental Health
Marov, Mikhail Ya., Department Chief, M. V. Keldysh Institute of

Applied Mathematics, Soviet Academy of Sciences, Moscow; Professor of Planetary Physics, Moscow State University

Meselson, Matthew, Thomas Dudley Cabot Professor of the Natural Sciences and Professor of Biochemistry and Molecular Biology, Harvard University

Minsky, Marvin L., Donner Professor of Science and Former Director, Artificial Intelligence Laboratory, Massachusetts Institute of Technology

Morimoto, Masaki, Director, Nobeyama Radio Observatory, Tokyo, Japan

Morrison, Philip, Institute Professor, Massachusetts Institute of Technology

Murray, Bruce, Professor of Geological and Planetary Science, California Institute of Technology; Former Director, Jet Propulsion Laboratory, NASA

Newman, William I., Assistant Professor of Planetary Physics and Astronomy, University of California, Los Angeles

Oliver, Bernard M., Vice President for Research and Development (Ret.), Hewlett-Packard Corporation

Oort, J. H., Professor of Astronomy, Leiden University; Former Director, Leiden Observatory, Netherlands; Past President, International Astronomical Union

Öpik, Ernst J., Senior Scientist, Armagh Observatory, Armagh, Northern Ireland, U.K.

Orgel, Leslie F., Research Professor, The Salk Institute; Adjunct Professor of Chemistry, University of California, San Diego

Pacini, Franco, Director, Arcetri Observatory, Florence, Italy

Papagiannis, Michael D., Chairman, Department of Astronomy, Boston University; President, Commission on the Search for Extraterrestrial Life, International Astronomical Union

Pauling, Linus, Former Chairman, Division of Chemistry and Chemical Engineering, California Institute of Technology; Chairman of the Board, Linus Pauling Institute of Science and Medicine; Nobel Laureate in Chemistry; Nobel Laureate in Peace; International Lenin Peace Prize Laureate; National Medal of Science

Pešek, Rudolf, Professor of Fluid Mechanics Emeritus, Faculty of Mechanical Engineering, Czech Technical University, Prague; Chairman, Commission on Astronautics, Czechoslovak Academy of Sciences

Pickering, W. H., Professor of Electrical Engineering Emeritus, California Institute of Technology; Former Director, Jet Propulsion Laboratory, NASA; National Medal of Science

Ponnamperuma, Cyril, Professor of Chemistry and Director, Laboratory of Chemical Evolution, University of Maryland

Purcell, Edward M., Gade University Professor Emeritus, Harvard University; Nobel Laureate in Physics; National Medal of Science

Raup, David M., Chairman, Department of Geophysical Sciences,

University of Chicago; Former Dean of Science, Field Museum of Natural History; Former Professor of Geology and Paleontology, University of Rochester
Reber, Grote, Inventor of the Radiotelescope; Tasmania
Rees, Martin J., Plumian Professor of Astronomy and Director of the Institute of Astronomy, Cambridge University, Cambridge, U.K.
Russell, Dale A., Chief, Paleobiology Division, National Museums of Canada, Ottawa, Canada
Sagdeev, Roald Z., Director, Institute for Cosmic Research, Soviet Academy of Sciences, Moscow
Shannon, Claude E., Former Research Mathematician, Bell Laboratories; Donner Professor of Science Emeritus, Massachusetts Institute of Technology, National Medal of Science
Shklovskii, I. S., Chairman, Astrophysics Division, Institute for Cosmic Research, Soviet Academy of Sciences, Moscow
Tarter, Jill, Research Astronomer, University of California, Berkeley
Thomas, Lewis, Chancellor, Memorial Sloan-Kettering Cancer Center, Professor of Medicine, Cornell University Medical School
Thorne, Kip S., William R. Kenan, Jr. Professor, and Professor of Theoretical Physics, California Institute of Technology
Troitsky, V. S., Scientific Director, Radiophysics Research Institute, Gorky, USSR
von Hoerner, Sebastian, Senior Staff Member, National Radio Astronomy Observatory
Wilson, Edward O., Baird Professor of Science and Professor of Biology, Harvard University, National Medal of Science
Zuckerman, Benjamin, Professor of Astronomy, University of Maryland

[Affiliations are for identification purposes only]

Contents

1 · "Innumerable Suns . . . Infinite Earths" 1

2 · Our Galactic Neighborhood 11

3 · Through the Milky Way . . . and Beyond! 22

4 · All the Spare Parts Needed for Life 32

5 · Life as We Don't Know It 42

6 · Have They Walked Among Us? 51

7 · Searching for the Main Street of the Universe 63

8 · The Rolls of the Cosmic Dice 82

9 · Where's My House Key? 91

10 · "We Are Made of Starstuff!" 101

    GLOSSARY 110

    BIBLIOGRAPHY 117

    INDEX 119

An aerial view of the world's largest radio telescope located near Arecibo, Puerto Rico. The giant reflecting surface is 1000 feet in diameter. The Arecibo Observatory is part of the National Astronomy & Ionosphere Center, which is operated by Cornell University under contract with the National Science Foundation.

ONE

"Innumerable Suns . . . Infinite Earths"

The air was filled with the steady hum of the motors that powered the giant radio telescope. The dish-shaped antenna was pointed at a tiny speck of starlight that moved slowly across the sky. At the focus of the antenna, there was an ultrasensitive radio receiver. It was capturing radio energy, amplifying it, then sending it down to the electronic detectors in the control room.

Inside that control room, the lights on the board were winking on and off in what seemed a random fashion. At the same time, the dials on the console panel revolved in their leisurely manner while the pens of the chart recorder moved over strips of paper. The painstakingly traced, ragged lines rose and fell depending on the amount of radio energy that was collected by the antenna. The emerging pattern was being intently studied by a small group of scientists.

The leader of these scientists was Dr. Frank Drake, a radio astronomer. The small gathering was part of a larger group, the members of which included an investigator into the origins of earthly life and a man who was studying the "language" of dolphins. This diverse mix of specialists had come together for a common purpose in 1960 in the mountains of Green Bank, West Virginia.

The gathering wasn't a top secret one, but each of the men had taken some care to avoid publicity. Despite their great personal faith in their project, they felt that it might not be taken seriously by other scientists. Some of their peers had not hesitated to say that the group was wasting its time. A few of them resented the use of the Green Bank radio telescope's valuable research hours for what they termed a "foolish endeavor."

One Russian scientist was asked whether or not his country was planning an investigation into this particular field. "If I proposed anything of the sort," he replied, "my government would think I was out of my mind."

The members of the Green Bank group had named their investigation Project Ozma, after the queen of the mythical land of Oz. The fanciful name was an indication that even they recognized that their work might be based more on elements of speculation than on facts.

What was the purpose of the controversial Project Ozma? What did the members of this group want to accomplish? By studying the distant stars, Tau Ceti and Epsilon Eridani, they hoped they might detect a significant change in the lines on the chart recorder.

If such a change occurred, the scientists would wait to see if it happened again and then again. If that particular signal kept on appearing, it would provide an answer to a question that had been puzzling human beings since the dawn of thought. It would prove for the first time that there is advanced life in interstellar space. It would prove that we earthlings are not alone in the universe.

Long before human beings began to record their history, they were speculating about their universe. Our ancestors stood upon mountaintops, on seashores, and on grassy plains, marveling at the countless twinkling points of light that became visible as darkness crept over the land.

Some thought the stars were the campfires of the gods. Others believed they were bright objects fastened to a rotating sphere that enclosed the universe. Still others thought the stars were merely pinholes in that sphere. Through these holes could be seen glimpses of the eternal fire that burned in the heavens beyond.

Our ancestors watched the moon rise from its home beyond the horizon. What is it? they may have wondered. Why is it there? What does it mean to us? Perhaps they also wondered why the moon evolved from a thin crescent into a full flat disc, then back into a crescent again in a regular endless pattern.

They came to depend upon the rhythmic lunar cycle, just as they depended upon the sun's appearance each dawn. On very rare occasions, however, a mysterious object crept over the sun, erasing its light long before nightfall. At those times, terrified tribesmen trembled, while their leaders exhorted the gods to release their sun from the clutches of darkness. The gods always seemed to answer their prayers. Within a short span of time, the brightness of the sunlight returned, and the people relaxed until the next solar eclipse occurred.

As time passed, people all over the world saw other signs of order in the sky. The "wanderers"—the five visible planets—appeared to follow predictable, although different, paths. Stars, in contrast, remained fixed in place with respect to each other. Their careless scattered locations offended the human eye. To satisfy their need for order, those who studied the stars grouped them into constellations. By stretching their imaginations to the limit, they traced out a beehive, a water carrier, a hunter, a huge bear, and various other objects, beasts, and personages.

The human interpretation of the cosmos varied from place to place and from tribe to tribe, but one belief was common to all—the earth was located in the center of the universe. Not only did it occupy the most favored position, but it operated under laws that existed nowhere else. Earth, for instance, was surely the only place that had the conditions that were suitable for the formation and support of life. This belief made earth superior to all other celestial bodies and allowed humankind to think of itself as unique.

For a long time, people enjoyed this feeling of being one of a kind. During the centuries just before Christ was born, however, a few philosophers began to try to expand their understanding of the universe. Are we really alone? they asked. Perhaps the stars are in reality other suns. In that case, there may be thousands of other planets. Why should earth be the only one that's inhabited? Would the gods stop with the creation of only one populated world? Isn't it reasonable to assume that they not only could, but *would*, create many more?

"To consider the earth as the only populated world in infinite space is as absurd as to assert that in an entire field sown with millet, only one grain will grow," said Metrodorus, a Greek philosopher in the fourth century B.C.

The simplest farmer could have understood that down-to-earth statement. The problem was that in those days, and during the centuries that followed, most people could not read. They knew only what they saw with their own eyes, and what they were told by their local religious and political leaders. Most educated people followed the teachings of Aristotle, who believed that the earth was located at the center of the universe and was the only place where life could possibly exist. Aristotle died in 322 B.C., but hundreds of years later he was still considered the absolute authority on scientific theory.

Alexander the Great was one of Aristotle's most famous students. After his sweeping military victories, someone dared to suggest that he might have conquered only one of several populated worlds. Alexander was angered by this "insane statement."

As time passed, more and more people began to question the wisdom of Aristotle in this matter. A few philosophers believed that invisible seeds of life were scattered throughout the universe. Whenever these spores found a suitable environment, they sprouted and flourished. Lucretius, a Roman who was born in the first century before Christ, was one of those who believed that life on Earth had arisen through natural processes that could easily occur in other parts of the universe.

"It is in the highest degree unlikely," he wrote, "that this earth and sky is the only one to have been created, and that all of those particles of matter outside are accomplishing nothing. As there are countless individuals in every species of animals, so there must be countless worlds and inhabitants thereof."

At about the same time, on the other side of the world, China's Teng Mu was telling his followers, "Empty space is like a kingdom, and the earth and sky are no more than a single individual in that kingdom."

The belief in extraterrestrial life continued to spread, but Aristotle's authority didn't start to crumble until the early 1500s. At that time, Copernicus proved that the sun, not the earth, was the center of our solar system, and that the earth was only one of several bodies that revolved around the sun. A few years later, Giordano Bruno went a few steps further. He said that the stars were actually "innumerable suns, and an infinite number of earths revolve around those suns. . . ." Bruno believed that countless numbers of beings inhabited those earths.

Church officials did their best to convince Bruno that he should retract his heretical statements. He refused and, after six months of imprisonment, was burned at the stake.

Bruno's death didn't dampen the fire that had been ignited in the minds of thinking persons throughout the western world. In the early 1600s Christian Huygens, a Dutch astronomer, looked through a telescope, a new tool that had been invented by Galileo. He saw that the other planets were not just points of light. They were shaped like balls. They looked like other worlds. Huygens quickly became a champion of extraterrestrial life.

Authors such as Milton and Pope write about fictional beings who lived on other planets. In the late 1800s, Edmond Rostand wrote *A Trip to the Moon*. In that fantasy, his hero, Cyrano de Bergerac, tried to convince some lunar beings that he had come from the real world, and that the moon was really nothing but an earthly satellite. When the leaders of the moon-people threatened him with execution for making such unfounded statements, Cyrano said that he had been telling falsehoods. To make amends, he assured the moon people that he had been wrong—that *they* were the residents of the real world.

"At least," he added in a whisper. "that is what the Council finds it proper for you to believe." Unlike Bruno, the fictional Cyrano was allowed to live.

Rostand's moon-people were products of his imagination, but the French writer Fontanelle really believed there were beings who traveled through outer space on comets. He declared that the residents of Mercury "are so full of fire that they are absolutely mad," and that the inhabitants of Saturn "live very miserably, the sun seems to them to be a little pale star, whose light and heat cannot but be weak at so great a distance."

Writers aren't the only ones who had some wild ideas about extraterrestrial life. Despite the obvious difficulties involved in living on the sun, there were at least two imaginative astronomers who thought it might be inhabited. One of them theorized that sun spots are actually openings in a brilliant shell that surrounds the solar body. These openings, he surmised, could allow us to view the sun's interior and enable the solar residents to look out and admire other stars.

Other scientists offered some much less fanciful speculations. Konstantin Tsiolkovsky, the founder of Russian astronautics, wrote that he had little doubt that there are planets of all ages sprinkled throughout our galaxy. Upon some of them, he said, life is just beginning to evolve. Upon the older ones, the inhabitants are likely to have technologies far more advanced than ours. Perhaps some of these beings have managed to overcome the force of gravity. Tsiolkovsky believed they might have created a space colony or two.

"All the phases of the development of human beings may be found on the different planets," Tsiolkovsky said. "What humanity was like several thousand years ago, and what it will be like in a few million years . . . all this will be found in the planetary worlds."

For thousands of years, people have been theorizing, speculating, debating, and fantasizing about the mysteries of the universe. For most of that time, they had no tools other than their own eyes to use in their study of the sky. When Galileo invented the telescope, astronomers acquired an instrument with which they could begin the serious study of the planets and stars.

Dr. Frank Drake and the other members of the Project Ozma team were the first to use radio telescopes to try to solve the mystery of whether or not there is any intelligent extraterrestrial life. They listened to a rush of radio noises for one hundred and fifty hours and even experienced one suspenseful false alarm, but found no cosmic radio message. They weren't discouraged though. No one had expected the search to be quick and easy. As Dr. Drake pointed out, the "needle" for which they were looking was very small, and the cosmic "haystack" very, very big. But they *had* made a start. They *had* ventured away from their secure earthly back yard into the Milky Way, a galactic neighborhood with which they were only vaguely familiar.

The researchers who gathered in Green Bank were only a few of many scientists who had become fascinated by the idea of searching for intelligent extraterrestrial life. Even before that meeting, there had already been several scientific papers published on the subject. One of the most significant had been authored by Giuseppe Cocconi and Philip Morrison. It was their ideas that caused many other people to start thinking about the possibility of finding life among the stars. The search for extraterrestrial intelligence (SETI) began to be taken seriously.

The work of these pioneers paved the way for other searchers involving certain stars or groups of stars. SETI research is now being conducted not only in the United States, but also in Japan and Europe. The Soviet government's attitude has changed from one of extreme doubt to one of enthusiastic support. The small, unpublicized meeting of a few scientists in Green Bank has expanded into research that has sparked discussions, debates, investigations, and involvement all around the world.

TWO

Our Galactic Neighborhood

"Ten-nine-eight-seven-six-five-four-three-two-one!" The voice coming over the loudspeaker fades as the rocket engine ignites with a burst of flame. Billowing yellow-white clouds of steam erupt from the water pit that cools the launch pad, then a roar sweeps over the area. Seconds later, the spacecraft punctures the thin, low-lying cloud layer, and another voyage of cosmic exploration has begun.

From the unaided human eye, to the optical telescope, to radio telescope and finally to spacecraft—our advancing technology is constantly pushing back the curtain that's always blocked our view of the universe. Orbiting satellites are constantly sending back a wealth of information. Remote instruments, aided by computers, have probed the rusty surface of Mars. The Voyagers' cameras have taken close-up pictures of Jupiter and Saturn. If all goes well, in 1986, they'll be photographing the face of Uranus, and in 1989, the face of Neptune.

We now use earthbound and earth-orbiting telescopes to study cosmic bodies that lie far beyond the reach of today's spacecraft. With special tools, astronomers can measure X rays, ultraviolet rays, and infrared rays that filter down from outer space. They have photographed the light from stars the lie far across the galaxy and have located strange bright objects that appear to be located at the very edge of the known universe. Each of these "quasars" gives off the combined light of trillions of the brightest stars.

Using radio telescopes, astronomers have recorded radio noises that originated billions of trillions of miles from Earth. Some of these noises are the fading whispers of the explosion that is thought to have taken place billions of years ago when our universe was born.

Scientific tools may eventually help us find an intelligent extraterrestrial race. Meanwhile, by studying the development of stars and planets other than our own, we can learn more about how our Earth and Sun came into existence. We can try to piece together the cosmic puzzle to learn how life began on our planet.

Our Sun is only an average, middle-sized, middle-aged star. If it began life as other average stars do, its creation took place in a "nebula," a huge, rotating cloud of cosmic gas and dust. Over a long period of time, the cloud started to contract. As it did, the relentless force of gravity pulled much of its material toward its center.

As the contraction progressed, the cloud mass rotated faster and faster. It flattened out until it resembled a giant whirlpool. Within that whirlpool, there were several smaller eddies, or swirls of gas and dust.

The cloud continued to shrink, and more material settled at its center. The atoms at the core began to gyrate wildly, knocking against each other. The electron was stripped from the single proton that to-

The large spiral galaxy in the constellation Andromeda. Similar in size and shape to our own Milky Way Galaxy, it is one of our closest galactic neighbors despite its distance of two million light years. The bright spots above and below the galaxy are small satellite galaxies orbiting the large galaxy. The "speckles" scattered throughout the photograph are stars in our own galaxy. Mount Palomar Observatory photo

gether had formed the nuclei of hydrogen atoms. These fragments collided with each other and with other atoms. With each collision, energy was released. The drastic structural changes slowly raised the cloud's temperature. By the time the mass had shrunk to a diameter of only one million miles, the temperature at the center of the cloud was ten million degrees.

At this point, our Sun's nuclear fires ignited, and the contraction slowed, then stopped. Supported by the energy radiating from its core, the newly created star balanced itself and resisted the tendency to collapse under its own weight. It took on a reddish glow, the signal that a stellar infant had been born. Its birth process had taken a total of twenty million years.

As the Sun was being born, the cooler and less dense outer regions of the cloud were giving birth to the nine planets. Atoms collided and stuck together to form grains of solid material. Silicon, aluminum, iron, ice crystals, and rock fragments started to trace their own orbits around the developing sun. As eons passed, random collisions occurred between tiny particles of matter. Some of them stuck together. After large numbers of such collisions, nine "protoplanets" were formed. The ones that were farthest from the sun were composed mainly of gaseous material. The ones closest to the sun contained much solid material, but were enveloped by hydrogen and other gases.

As the sun entered its "teen-age" years, the heat and light from its nuclear reactions burned their way through the nebula. The atmospheres of the inner planets were swept away as the energy of the sun increased. By this time, the planets had grown so large that they were able to draw to them almost all of the remaining solid material in the nearby solar system. The scars of this bombardment can still be seen on our moon and on Mars and Mercury.

When the Earth finally reached its present size, it was nothing but a huge ball of rocky material with no water or air. That condition was soon to be changed. Within the new planet's depths, radioactive elements were disintegrating and slowly heating up the surrounding area. After several hundred million years, the internal temperature had reached thousands of degrees. The rock at the center of the earth was so hot that it melted. The molten materials expanded and rose toward the surface. These broke through the weak spots in the Earth's crust, and a flood of lava poured out. As these volcanoes erupted, they released trapped gases such as water vapor, hydrogen, methane, ammonia, and nitrogen. From these gases, a simple atmosphere was formed.

Earth is a very small planet. The outer planets, which are Jupiter, Saturn, Uranus, and Neptune, are much larger. Recent studies have shown that the atmospheres of Jupiter and Saturn may be much like the atmosphere of primitive Earth. It's not known whether they have a solid core underneath all the layers of swirling gaseous matter. It may be that Jupiter, at least, is so large, and has so much internal pressure causing heat, that it never cooled down enough to form a permanent, solid external crust.

In fact, if Jupiter had been much larger, it probably would have developed into a star. Our solar system would then have become one of the many binary star systems in our galaxy. A binary star system is one in which two neighboring stars are so close that they revolve around a common center of gravity.

Our sun is now about five billion years old. If it follows the same life cycle as other average stars, five billion more years will pass before it has used up all of its fuel. As its nuclear fire dies down and its core cools, it will become unstable and start to collapse.

For a while, this collapsing material will renew the sun's energy, and a blast of radiation will expand its outer layers like a balloon. The sun will then become a red giant. Its scorching heat will envelope Mercury and Venus, and the temperature on Earth will soar. The inner planets will soon become dead, scarred satellites orbiting a dying sun.

As the sun continues to fight for its life, it will start to shrink to retain its balance and thus prolong its life. Despite these frantic last-ditch efforts, its nuclear fire will eventually go out and its life will come to an end. It will become a shrunken white dwarf, about the size of Earth, but a thousand times denser than lead. Some White Dwarfs are so dense that a ton of their material could be put into a match box.

While the sun is going through its death throes, the outer planets will also be dying, their energy slowly seeping away. All of the nine dead planets will continue their endless orbiting of the Sun, which will eventually become nothing but a huge cinder. The group will wander aimlessly through the vastness of the Milky Way, until someday, millions of years in the future, it may be gathered into another nebula. Its material may then be recycled into other worlds and other suns.

Stars that have at least six times the mass of our sun stage a far more spectacular farewell. Such a performance takes place in our galaxy only once or twice every century. When a mammoth star collapses, its internal temperature suddenly climbs to billions of degrees. The tremendous heat causes a cataclysmic explosion. The star's outer layers are blasted into space with a force equal to that of billions upon billions of hydrogen bombs. The explosions of some "supernovas" are capable of ripping apart an entire planetary system.

In 1054 A.D. Chinese astronomers witnessed a very special supernova, which they called the "guest star." Its light was bright enough to be seen for many months, even in the daytime with the unaided eye. The remnants of this spectacular event can still be seen from Earth with telescopes, nine hundred years after the original occurrence.

When the explosion of a supernova is over, there may be nothing left at the site of the original star but gas. The debris has been scattered over millions of miles of space. Sometimes, however, there remains a small sphere of mashed material that was formed by the crushing pressure of the star's collapse. Within this sphere, the different atoms that existed in the original star are no longer distinguishable from one another. The individual electrons and protons have been compressed into neutrons. The supernova has evolved into a "neutron star," which contains most of the mass of a star that was once five hundred to a thousand times larger than our sun. The neutron star is one hundred million times smaller than the star from which it was formed. It has shrunk to the size of a ball only about ten miles in diameter.

Until 1967, astronomers had only suspected the existence of neutron stars. In that year, their theories were proven when Jocelyn Bell, a young Irish astronomy student, noticed a strange pointlike cosmic object. It gave out precisely timed radio signals once every one-and-one-third seconds. The timing of these sharp bursts of energy was more accurate than that of the most finely tuned digital clock.

Miss Bell knew she was observing a starlike object because its radio energy seemed to "twinkle." This apparent twinkle occurs when material in space interferes with the passage of either light or radio waves. Stars are so far away that they look like points. The light from these points twinkles as it passes through Earth's atmosphere. In contrast, our moon, which is so close to use, appears as a disk that does not twinkle. The planets of our solar system, seen through a telescope, also appear as untwinkling spheres with definite shapes.

Extremely distant sources of radio energy are

also seen as pointlike objects. Their radio waves twinkle as they pass through the material in the galaxy.

After Miss Bell's first observation, several research groups searched the sky to find the origins of the strange "beeping" radio signals. Could they possibly be the beacons of a fleet of starships? Were they messages from one galactic civilization to another? Were they signals that had been beamed toward our solar system in an attempt at communication? Scientists were elated at the possibility of finding an extraterrestrial civilization. They gave their discovery the whimsical name of LGM, which stands for Little Green Men.

Their elation was short-lived. It soon became clear that the signals were coming from some unknown but natural source. The mystery was solved when it was found that the object was a "pulsar," a type of rapidly spinning neutron star. As a pulsar spins, it gives out a stream of radiation that sweeps through space like a lighthouse beacon. As more pulsars were found, astronomers realized that each seemed to appear in an area where a supernova had been observed.

Scientific excitement mounted again. The theories and predictions about neutron stars had been proven by observation. These compact little stars are indeed the remains of giant stars. The mystery of the "guest star," which the Chinese had seen in 1054 A.D., was now finally being solved. Where that tremendously bright light had appeared in the constellation of Taurus the Bull, a pulsar was found.

Pulsars are so compact that if the entire earth were compressed to the same degree, it would be only 600 feet in diameter. A fragment of a pulsar the size of a sugar cube can weigh one billion tons, more than the combined weight of a fleet of battleships.

Astronomers used to believe that nothing could be more compact than a white dwarf. Then they discovered neutron stars. Now it's believed that there are objects in space that are more compact than neutron stars. According to the laws of physics, even the largest of stars could keep on shrinking while keeping most of its mass. Such a star could, in fact, keep shrinking until it had shrunk almost to oblivion. It could become just a black dot in the blackness of space, a point of nothingness, invisible because its gravity would be so strong that not even a ray of light could escape its pull. Anything that drew too close to one of these "black holes" would be sucked into it and disappear forever.

No one can see a black hole. Therefore it's difficult to prove that such an object exists. Would it have some sort of "signature" to let us know it's there? Researchers believe that an answer to that question has come from satellites equipped to measure the X rays that are found throughout interstellar space.

One intense and powerful source of X rays has been located in our own galaxy. Scientists have tried to explain the existence of these X rays in various ways. Nothing, however, fits all the known facts as well as a black hole. It's believed that this particular black hole was once one half of a binary star system. The companion star is now orbiting the black hole. The tremendous gravitational pull of the invisible object tears streamers of gas from its star neighbor. The gas rushes toward the boundary of the black hole. As its atoms collide during the hectic journey, intense bursts of X rays are produced.

It's difficult for human minds to grasp the idea of a black hole. Such objects are far beyond the realm of our experience. They are, however, only one of the fascinating puzzles that abound in our galactic neighborhood. What new riddles will appear? And which of them will we solve as we continue to explore the Milky Way? Will we find the clues that will eventually lead us to the discovery of extraterrestrial life?

THREE

Through the Milky Way . . . and Beyond!

"There's an uprising on Planet L-119 in the Beta Galaxy. Consult Cosmic Map number four-five-two-one, upper left quadrant for exact location. I'm organizing a strike force to subdue the rebels. We'll leave within the hour."

The commander of the fleet of starships finished his radio report to the Galactic Union Headquarters in the Andromeda Galaxy. He then gave a succession of orders to his lieutenant. Forty-five minutes later, the engines of his stellar craft were fired up, the members of his crew hurried to their stations, and the command to lift off was given. Everything proceeded in a smooth, orderly fashion. These intergalactic peacekeeping missions were becoming a part of everyday life.

This scene, or one like it, could appear in any one of hundreds of science fiction tales. In a writer's imagination, interstellar travel is commonplace. Futuristic astronauts zip about from planet to planet, from one group of stars to the next, and even from galaxy to galaxy with the greatest of ease. There are no speed limits. The starships glide across the cosmos at many times the speed of light.

Good science fiction writers tell exciting and absorbing stories. To keep the action going, however, they have to use our earthly concepts of time and distance. Their planets appear to be only an hour or so away from each other. Within a day or two, a group of astronauts can visit several planetary systems within the same galaxy. A week later, they may be exploring a neighboring galaxy. The writer has condensed the almost incomprehensible vastness of space into something that our minds can grasp.

Science fiction is stimulating and thought-provoking, but we must be careful not to confuse it with reality. We have to realize how microscopic we are in comparison to just *one* galaxy. Suppose our Milky Way were the size of the earth. On that scale, our entire solar system would be the size of a grapefruit. Our planet would be smaller than the smallest seed within that grapefruit. Our sun, which seems so huge to us, is only one average-sized star among the Milky Way's one hundred billion to two hundred fifty billion stars. Finally, to put everything in the proper perspective, we must realize that there are untold billions of galaxies in the visible universe. Each of them also contains billions of stars.

The distances in space are as difficult to understand as are the numbers of stars and galaxies. They are so great that a billion miles is only the first tiny step up a stairway that may never end. Astronomers are used to working with numbers so large that a few billion more or less often makes little difference. When we read in one newspaper that a new star was born fifty billion miles away, then read in another paper that the event was occurring fifty-three billion miles away, we might be confused. Actually, in terms of "astronomical accuracy" those two figures are very close. The difference between them is only six percent.

The men and women who study the skies find it difficult to use our earthly measurements of time and distance. They have had to develop a different sort of yardstick, one in which units of distance are compared to the distance light travels during a certain period of time. For example, light travels 186,000 miles per second, so the moon can be said to be a little more than a "light second" away from Earth. The sun is eight "light minutes" away from us. Saturn is one-and-one-third "light hours" distant, and Alpha Centauri, our nearest star neighbor, is four "light years" distant.

Our fastest moving, most modern spacecraft travel at only a tiny fraction of the speed of light. It might take one of them about one hundred thousand years to journey to one of the closest stars. If reaching a "nearby" point within our own galaxy is so difficult, then intergalactic travel presents problems that defy the imagination.

The Milky Way and the Andromeda Galaxy are located within our group of about two dozen galaxies. Millions upon millions of light years further down the cosmic road lie other galactic clusters. Beyond them, widely scattered throughout the universe, there are billions more. Astronomers recently discovered a string of galaxies that's 100 to 200 million light years away from us. It's 700 million light years long and stretches halfway across our sky.

Some galaxies look like our Milky Way, a gossamer spiral of stars rotating around a dense, bright nucleus. These galaxies contain a mixture of stars in all stages of formation from the youngest to the oldest.

Many galaxies are irregular in shape, and others are elliptical. Some are rich in cosmic gas and dust, from which many new stars are being formed. Others may have used up most of these materials and are less likely to become stellar nurseries.

An odd thing happens when astronomers look across the expanse of space to study galaxies and other cosmic phenomena. Their telescopes are collecting light that has traveled billions or even trillions of miles. In the case of a quasar, the light could have taken billions of years to reach our solar system. Thus, the image that we see is not the object as it would appear if it were close to us. The object is seen as it looked in the distant past, long before our earth was created. When human beings peer into their telescopes, they're not only looking across great distances. They are also looking backward in time, playing the cosmic movie in reverse.

In the same manner, through the "ears" of a radio telescope, radio astronomers can pick up the faint murmurs of a supernova explosion that occurred long ago in some far corner of our galaxy. If

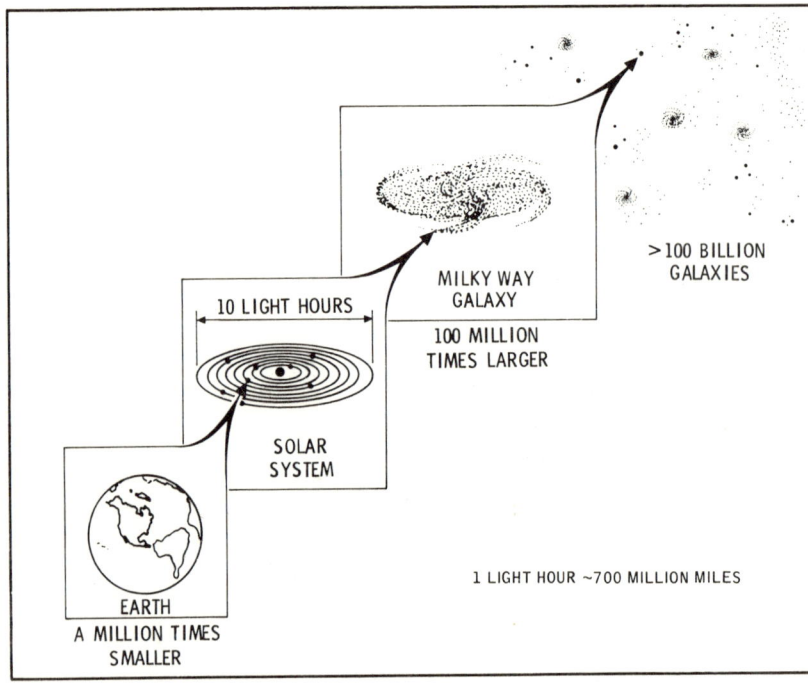

Our relationship to the universe. From this figure we see that our earth is a million times smaller than our solar system, which in turn is 100 million times smaller than our Milky Way Galaxy. As big as our galaxy is, it is just one of a huge number of galaxies, more than 100 thousand million, that make up the universe as we know it. Courtesy JPL/Caltech

their instruments could pick up the sights and sounds of the beginning of the universe, what would they discover?

According to one widely accepted idea, the Big Bang theory, the universe did not always exist as we know it. There may have once been just silent, black emptiness. Within that void, there may have been a single object, a "cosmic egg," the embryo of the universe. According to the Big Bang theory, this pea-sized, enormously dense "super drop" contained all of the energy and matter that now exists.

Researchers estimate that between ten and twenty billion years ago, at "time zero," this super-drop blew apart in the most gigantic explosion that's ever occurred. Within a tiny fraction of a second, our entire universe burst into existence.

During the first 1/1000 of the first second, the infant universe consisted of nothing but tremendously hot radiation, then electrons and strange sub-atomic particles called "quarks" appeared. The quarks were destined to be the building blocks of protons, but in this first split second after time zero, it was still too hot for them to survive. All of the particles were quickly snuffed out by the intense radiation that surrounded them. The process could be compared to the obliteration of trees and houses in an earthly fire-storm.

When the universe was almost one second old, it had already cooled to a "mere" 150 billion degrees. This drop in temperature was an important milestone in cosmic history. At this point, electrons could survive, and trios of quarks were frozen into protons and neutrons. Quarks have never since been found in a free state because the temperatures in nature are far too cool.

At time zero plus three minutes, the universe had cooled off enough to allow neutrons and protons to join to form the nuclei of future atoms. Now the universe consisted of atomic nuclei and free electrons swimming in a sea of hot radiation.

The cosmos continued to expand and cool. When five hundred thousand years had passed, the positively charged nuclei began to capture the negatively charged electrons. The electrons began to orbit the nuclei. The simplest of all atoms, hydrogen and helium, came into existence. Hydrogen has only one electron and one proton, while helium has two electrons, two protons, and two neutrons. These bits of material became the basis for everything the universe now contains. Hydrogen still accounts for ninety-eight percent of all matter in existence today.

Atoms and molecules gradually became more abundant and gravity began to pull some of this matter into great clumps. In this way, the first galaxies started to form. A billion years later, within galactic clouds of hydrogen and helium gas, the first stars were born. Within these stars were forged the heavier elements, such as carbon, nitrogen, oxygen, calcium and iron.

The force of the Big Bang was so tremendous that even today cosmic bodies and materials are hurtling away from each other in all directions. The recently discovered galactic string appears to be speeding toward the outer edge of the universe at about 3,000 miles per second. Quasars, which are currently believed to be the most far flung and most ancient remnants of the Big Bang, are still moving away, still expanding the boundaries of the universe. One recently discovered quasar is about twelve billion light years away from Earth. Distances within the universe and between celestial bodies, already so enormous, are constantly growing even greater.

Until recent times, we humans have been locked in a cocoon formed by our limited sense of time and distance. We're now finding that there are areas in which days, years, and centuries, inches, feet, and miles have very little meaning. Physicists are probing the mysteries of subatomic particles, which are smaller than anything ever before imagined. At the same time, our exploration of space is continuing to reveal the awesome nature and size of the universe.

Will the story of the cosmos ever be fully told? No one knows, because that story is extremely complex, and it's just beginning to unfold. The Big Bang theory provides a few answers, but it doesn't quite fit all the known facts. To provide a more complete explanation, a new version of the theory has been introduced.

With the "inflationary theory," scientists attempt to picture exactly how the Big Bang looked in the first few trillionths of a trillionth of a trillionth of a second after time zero. During that incredibly tiny split second, according to this new idea, the "bang" became a "pffft," and a foam consisting of bubbles of energy appeared. One of these bubbles ballooned to the size of an orange. That bubble continued to expand and cool, just as it did according to the original Big Bang theory. The process resulted in the universe that we now see all around us.

What happened to the other bubbles in the space foam? Did they balloon into other universes, separated from ours by walls of energy? If so, our universe may be only one of many that exist within a "super universe."

So far, no single theory has explained everything we need to know about the creation of our universe. The ongoing search for the truth can be compared to the search for a long lost trail. To find the beginning of that trail, researchers must first clear away piles of accumulated brush and rubble, the superstitions and misconceptions that have grown up over the centuries.

As they inch forward, they'll come to some parts of the trail that have been washed out, because the passage of time has destroyed important evidence. Perhaps some of those gaps will never be filled in, but new knowledge can help to bridge them or tie them together. There will probably be times when the researchers will reach a dead end, and the theory they've been using will have to be discarded. They'll have to back up until they're once again standing on firm ground, and then work on a new group of ideas.

During the search, scientists will stumble upon

small sections of the trail, bits of knowledge that will convince them they're on the right track. Each proven fact will be added to the growing accumulation of knowledge.

Through the combined efforts of people all over the world, the various parts of the cosmic story may someday fall into place. At that time, the lost trail will have been found.

FOUR

All the Spare Parts Needed for Life

Our earth was born about four or five billion years ago. During the first billion years, an almost constant volcanic activity kept pushing molten rock to the surface. As this activity slowed down, the infant planet cooled, and the molten material began to harden. Eventually, the earth's crust became firm. Some parts were light and thick. They floated on the molten material below and became continents. During this time, the atmosphere also cooled down. As it did, water vapor condensed and the first rains fell on the earth. This water drained into the heavier, but thinner, crustal regions, and the oceanic basins were formed.

At the beginning of the earth's second billion years, the young sun was radiating only about half the light and heat it would later produce. At this time, the earth's atmosphere was constantly chilly. It was composed mainly of hydrogen combined with the pungent fumes of ammonia and the odorless

All the Spare Parts Needed for Life · 33

menace of methane. There were only a few traces of oxygen.

The continuing rains caused a shallow sea to cover much of the surface of the planet. A few more hundreds of millions of years passed, and occasional volcanic eruptions wracked the seafloor. In some places, layer after layer of lava grew into mounds so high they rose above the water's surface. Those mounds were the beginnings of our islands. At that time, however, all of the primitive island and continents were nothing but clumps of bare rock, untouched by greenery.

How did those bleak surfaces become covered with plants and animals? What events caused the sea to become a breeding ground for living things ranging from microscopic plankton to whales? Scientists aren't certain, because the start of the trail that led to earthly life was destroyed long ago. Bits and pieces of evidence have been collected by generations of scientists, but there are still many gaps in our knowledge. We may never be able to bridge those gaps unless we find another planet upon which life is just beginning to form.

Meanwhile, scientists are searching for clues here on earth. They have patched together a chain of events that could have been the faltering steps that led to the formation of life. It begins with a series of thunderstorms that lashed our planet when it was young. With each flash of lightning, new combinations of atoms were formed by the fusing of methane, ammonia, water, and hydrogen. Molecules such as "amino acids" and "nucleotides," the building blocks of living cells, were created.

Succeeding rains washed the molecules into the sea. Carbon dioxide and other compounds that dissolve in liquid water were carried to the earth's wet surface. Streams flowed over rocks, wore them down, then carried the dissolved salts and minerals into the sea. The world's oceans were becoming rich, warm soups of organic matter.

Winds and tides moved the molecules about in this soup. Many of them collided, and sometimes they stuck together to form larger molecules. After a while, another molecule joined them, then another, and another. Some of the molecule collections were weak and unstable, so they soon broke up. The strong, stable ones continued to develop and became skilled at attracting still more members to their colony.

One theory suggests that some of the amino acids became absorbed on the surfaces of clay deposits or concentrated in tidal pools. In these close quarters, they had the chance to link themselves together in long chains. By the time a billion more years had passed, random collisions and the growth of amino acids in pools and upon clays had resulted in bits of matter of varying shapes and sizes. Some were long, thin strands. Others were wound into tight clumps. Still others were twisted into spirals.

Some molecular colonies developed better ways to draw into themselves an increasing amount of the sea's dissolved organic compounds. As millions of years passed, there wasn't enough of this "food" to sustain the very large molecule population. The first struggle for existence began.

In order to better compete for the sea's raw materials, one type of molecule developed the ability to copy itself. These "replicating" molecules soon dominated the waters of the earth. Their appearance marked the crossing of an important evolutionary threshold.

As the competition among molecules increased, a few of the colony types survived by developing specialized cells. Some of the cells digested food. Others were sensitive to light, or to vibrations, or to traces of different chemicals in the water. Another type had a harder than usual outer membrane, or skin.

Finally, out of all the countless meetings of billion upon billions of different kinds of molecules; out of all the mixing of chemical elements; out of all the forms and shapes of molecular colonies, the essence of life appeared upon Earth. By the time our planet was about one billion years old, life had gained a hesitant foothold upon its surface.

As more and more tiny bits of living matter swarmed in the sea, the water protected them from the deadly force of the sun's ultraviolet rays. Within this liquid blanket, microbes, algae, and wormlike creatures were able to thrive. Eventually, these organisms became divided into two distinct groups. One had the characteristics of plants, the other the properties of animals. Some of the plantlike organisms took in carbon dioxide and produced oxygen as a waste product. This gas accumulated in the atmosphere. Here it met the ultraviolet rays that come from our sun. The ultraviolet rays used up most of their energy breaking up the oxygen molecules, which then regrouped to form the ozone molecule, which contains three oxygen atoms. This ozone layer acted as a barrier that prevented the ultraviolet rays from continuing their journey to the surface of the earth.

Since the threat from ultraviolet rays was now greatly reduced, some living things began to cluster near the sea's surface. By the time the earth was two billion years old, its atmosphere contained a significant amount of oxygen. A few creatures ventured out of the water onto the land. Plants, insects, and spiders invaded the islands and continents. Only the hardiest of these survived, because the land was still a much more hostile place than the sea.

Many of those that endured did so because they developed a new kind of cell that used oxygen as a fuel. Since oxygen supplies quick energy, these organisms became much more skilled than others at seeking food and retreating from danger. That same fuel gave their brain cells the abundant energy that's needed for thought.

Over millions of years, larger and more varied forms of life appeared. There came a time when one species of huge reptiles came to dominate the Earth. The dinosaur's brain, as small as it was, gave it a tremendous advantage over the nonthinking creatures.

The dinosaurs mysteriously perished seventy million years ago. After their disappearance, another long series of events took place that led to the appearance of a new species. This species had a large brain. It was able to fashion tools, to plan for its future, and, eventually, to stand erect. These special qualities set it above all other species, enabling it to survive in a world that was full of violence and danger. Without those qualities, human beings may long ago have gone the way of the dinosaur.

What happened during the time that passed between the disappearance of the dinosaurs and the appearance of humankind? This great gap in the trail is still puzzling scientists as much as the gaps that remain in our knowledge of the beginning of life. At this time, there are only theories about both these unknown events and the amount of time they took. There are some who believe that a divine force created all forms of life in a very short time. Others believe that a bombardment of meteoroids and comets could have brought the early preformed organic compounds into our atmosphere. Still another group thinks that earthly life was seeded by alien visitors or by meteorites from outer space. The question here, of course, is where did *those* seeds come from? Just how did *they* get their spark of life?

Laboratory experiments have given support to the believers in "spontaneous generation," the creation of living matter from nonliving matter. The problem is that one important ingredient is always missing from any man-made formula. That ingredient is time. Nature took hundreds of millions of years to produce and develop life upon this planet. Individual scientists, in contrast, may calculate, extrapolate, and estimate, but their laboratory tests are limited to hours, months, or just a few years. Although they are building on the work of previous generations, and the collection of data continues to grow over decades, researchers have yet to create life in a laboratory.

The searchers for extraterrestrial life are concerned about how life began here on earth. Everything they learn about that subject will help them to understand whether life is a very rare occurrence, or whether it would arise wherever the conditions are right. Did the first cells develop haphazardly entirely through random collisions? Or was there some master blueprint by which the process was directed?

The collisions between all those molecules may indeed have occurred by chance. But why did some of them form stable colonies, while others didn't? Perhaps the development of life was influenced by the natural preferences that some chemical elements have for each other.

Chance may also have played a role as life evolved into more and more intelligent species. Nevertheless, it appears that the natural law of the survival of the fittest had much to do with the process. Other natural laws no doubt influenced the formation of increasingly complex and efficient organisms.

If the appearance of life was nothing but an accident, what are the chances of it happening again somewhere else? Is life likely to be created whenever there is enough time and the conditions are suitable?

Some people think so. "Imagine a planet made up entirely of the components of watches," one writer said. "Given enough time—a thousand million years or so—tidal forces and the movements of winds will assemble at least one working watch."

Logic tells us that without a plan of some sort, the chances are greatly against a watch being produced in such a haphazard manner. On the other hand, what if there *were* a master plan at work? Little by little, as eons passed, the parts of the watch would inevitably come together in just the right order. In the case of the development of life, the laws of nature would be set down in such a way that they would heavily weight the odds in favor of success.

At this point, we don't know whether or not there is a blueprint for life. If we could find just one more inhabited planet, that discovery might give new clues to indicate that there may be such a master plan. It would certainly encourage the searchers for extraterrestrial life. Meanwhile, they continue to base their belief in their work on the many facts that have been proven to be true.

It's known, for instance, that the ingredients necessary for life exist throughout the Milky Way.

Our galaxy has, in fact, been described as a storehouse full of the spare parts needed for life. Hydrogen, carbon, nitrogen, oxygen and sulphur are only a few of the atoms found in several dozen types of molecules that radio astronomers have found in the clouds of gas and dust in which stars are forming. Each of these molecules has been positively identified by its unique "fingerprint," the amount of energy it emits and absorbs at different specific wavelengths.

From time to time, evidence that these chemicals have developed into more complex molecules has been found. Some of this evidence has literally fallen from the sky in the form of meteorites. Most of these rocky, metallic chunks of material don't contain any clues, but one variety called a "carbonaceous chondorite" does. One of these extremely rare meteorites fell on Kentucky in 1950, and another landed in Australia in 1969. Fortunately, both were seen as they plunged to earth, so they didn't get lost. Scientists rushed to the sites and examined them before the meteorites became contaminated with foreign substances.

These two objects fell on opposite sides of the world, nineteen years apart, but they were remarkably alike. Both contained traces of water plus small quantities of the amino and fatty acids that are found in the protein of living tissues. This discovery was proof that somewhere, millions of miles from Earth, simple chemicals had been combined into complex molecules.

Given the right conditions, could some of these

molecules evolve into living creatures as they did on Earth? Could the history of life be repeated again and again? If so, our galaxy could contain civilizations in all stages of development. Our chances of eventually contacting one of them would be high.

Or will these molecules in space remain as they are? Is life on earth a random thing that has little chance of occurring anywhere else? If that's true, we may be alone in the universe. If we are unique, then the human race is more valuable than anyone every imagined.

Whatever the answers to those questions, they will affect all of humankind and the way we feel about ourselves and our place in the galaxy.

FIVE

Life as We Don't Know It

What form is extraterrestrial life likely to take? If living cells appear elsewhere, and if complex organisms evolve from those cells, do they always develop into life as we know it? Or could they develop into life as we *don't* know it?

Science fiction writers have been giving us imaginative answers to those questions for a long time. Among the most famous extraterrestrials are the characters in H. G. Wells's *The War of the Worlds*. "There were huge bodies—or rather heads—about four feet in diameter, each having in front of it a face. This face had no nostrils—indeed, the Martians do not seem to have a sense of smell—but it had a pair of very large dark colored eyes, and just beneath this, a kind of fleshy beak.... In a group around the mouth were sixteen slender, almost whiplike tentacles, arranged in two bunches of eight each."

Other writers have described extraterrestrials as blue flames, or simply as forces, with no apparent physical form. Venusians have been said to be grotesque and hostile bug-eyed monsters, in keeping with their environment. In contrast, other alien beings are said to look like perfectly formed earthlings, with serene dispositions. Still others, such as the title character in the movie *E.T.*, are lovable, intelligent, and peaceful little creatures.

Some people have claimed to have seen extraterrestrials here on Earth. They have given widely varying descriptions of them. Such sightings were reported as far back as Biblical times and are still being reported today.

"They looked like green goblins," one man said, "with bulging eyes on the sides of their heads, short bodies with long arms, and clawlike fingers. There were wide slits for mouths and pointed ears."

Another alien visitor was described as being about three feet tall with a large head and round, protruding eyes like "large yellow-green plums."

Extraterrestrials have been said to have pincers for fingers and eyes like lighted flashlight bulbs; as being bristly and short, or tall with shoulder-length blond hair; or entirely hairless with no neck and an underdeveloped body. Some were said to stand upright, while others scurried about on all fours. They were handsome, monsterlike, fishlike, ghoullike, and godlike.

What if some or all of these reports are true? If they are, we must have been visited by beings from a great number of galactic worlds. There must also be a wide range of forms in which intelligent life can be found.

Writers are free to use their imaginations. Anyone can claim to have seen an extraterrestrial visitor. Scientists, on the other hand, can't base their work upon fantasy. They must find proof that goes beyond eyewitness reports that may or may not be reliable. They have to depend upon known facts and the results of many tests.

So far, no one has produced any solid physical evidence of even one extraterrestrial visitation. Since there is no proof that any human being has ever seen an alien being, no one can say with certainty just what form an alien life may take.

To gain a better understanding of this mystery, the science of "exobiology" has emerged. Exobiologists try to understand how life might begin and grow far from earth. To make this study meaningful, they must first understand how life starts. They are seeking the answers to many questions. Is life plentiful throughout the galaxy, or is it rare? Can life begin in interstellar space, or does it have to start on a planet? How does life evolve from the simplest forms to the very complex?

Exobiologists know that the "stuff" of life is out there in space. But how do those raw materials *become* life?

One of the questions an exobiologist must answer is: What, exactly, *is* life? On just one planet—our earth—it takes four million different forms, and includes everything from the simplest organisms to plants, animals, and human beings. A tree is alive, and so is a cockroach, but neither bears any resemblance to the other. A bacteria is unlike a whale. A dog could never be mistaken for a sea urchin or a petunia. And yet all of these things are said to be alive.

Despite these great differences, there are some characteristics that all earthly life has in common. One is the ability to reproduce, to make copies of itself. Another is the ability to take in nourishment and to give off waste. Still more common characteristics are found in the molecules of all known living things. A blade of grass, an elephant, a spider, and a human being all use DNA to pass along their hereditary traits, and they all have some of the same types of enzymes.

Since these characteristics are shared by so many different living things on earth, many researchers agree that they may also form the basis of extraterrestrial life. Those same people, however, may disagree about the conditions under which life could evolve. They know it could occur on a planet that is much like earth. But what about one that is much less dense than earth, one that has a very low gravity and a thin atmosphere? If life existed there, it would certainly be influenced by those conditions.

What if a planet was much colder than earth? Our planet's moderate temperature allows millions of molecular interactions to take place at a rapid pace. In a cold atmosphere, those interactions would be much less frequent, so life might evolve much more slowly. As the creatures developed, their chemical and biological activities would also be slow. Under those circumstances, would there be much chance of intelligent beings arising?

What if a planet had all but one of the elements that we believe are necessary for life? On earth, carbon forms the "backbone" of large molecules in living matter. Could silicon replace carbon in the cells of another type of being? Science fiction writers have written about silicon based creatures living in furnace temperatures and thinking at lightning speed. Biologists aren't convinced that such beings could exist.

Sulphur atoms and oxygen atoms are alike in some ways. Could sulphur replace oxygen in the cells of a living creature? Until recently, most scientists would have answered no to that question. Not long ago, however, oceanographers discovered some giant worms living near a cluster of volcanic vents on the seafloor. They seem to thrive in temperatures that are far above the normal boiling point of water. They exist in a chemical environment that would kill most living cells. In addition to those startling characteristics, these worms appear to use sulphur instead of oxygen in their metabolic processes. Is it possible that somewhere in our galaxy there's a very hot planet that's inhabited by sulphur based life?

Despite the possible differences in planetary conditions, some biologists believe that the basic design of an extraterrestrial would be much like that of a human being. They see great advantages in walking on two legs, having a central brain located in one head, and in having two eyes that are both focused in the same direction.

There are others who disagree with this idea. "It would be sheer conceit on our part to maintain that we are the ideal mode," argued one of them. "The suggestion that somewhere in the universe there may be a race of people with three heads and a dozen legs is not necessarily absurd."

There really is little reason to believe that advanced extraterrestrial beings would resemble human beings at all. Our own biological evolution didn't progress along a smooth, direct arc, like the route of a jet airplane from Los Angeles to New York. It probably more closely resembled the meanderings of a confused white mouse in a maze. The development of earthly life was more than likely filled with detours, dead ends, and unexpected twists and turns. The only fact that's really known is that it was guided by natural laws. Just how precisely it was guided is what is not known.

It's interesting to think about what would have happened if one of the chance events along our evolutionary path hadn't occurred. What if life had "zigged" rather than "zagged" at one or more important crossroads?

What might have happened, for instance, if the dinosaurs hadn't been eliminated by a catastrophic event that took place sixty-five million years ago? One type of these reptiles was more intelligent than the others. Would it have eventually learned to co-operate in the hunting of other creatures? If so, human beings might not have had the chance to evolve, multiply, and become the dominant species on this planet. In that case, at this time, a four-legged, long-necked creature with millions of years of evolution behind it might be ruling the Earth. It might have developed an intelligence much greater than ours. It might be doing more than just wondering about the possibility of communicating with extraterrestrial life. Would that creature have long ago hooked into a network of communicating minds across the cosmos? Would it have built a starship that could carry it from one solar system to another?

If intelligent extraterrestrial beings are likely to be so different from us, is there much of a chance that they might transmit messages that we can understand? The well-known astronomer, Carl Sagan, thinks there is. He says it's not what an extraterrestrial *looks* like that's important. It's what it *knows* that counts.

It's probably safe to say that wherever life occurs, the beings with the largest brains in proportion to their body size will come to rule over the other species. Their intelligence will enable them to think, then to investigate their immediate surroundings. Sooner or later, they'll start to probe the mysteries of their galactic neighborhood, just as we are starting to do. And, just as we have, they will be likely to ask the question, "Is there any intelligent life in outer space?"

As these extraterrestrial beings live their lives, they'll have to come to grips with the same laws of nature that rule us, because those laws exist everywhere in the universe. Their quest for knowledge may take them down many of the paths along which we are now traveling. An extraterrestrial's biology, psychology, sociology, and politics may be very different from ours. Nevertheless, the numbers "one, two, three" and the laws of mathematics will have the same meaning. For instance, the relationship between the diameter of a circle and its circumference is the same in all parts of the galaxy. To a race living on a distant planet, the Milky Way would look the same as it does to us, except for a variation in the patterns of the closest stars.

"I would certainly not expect an extraterrestrial's brain to be anatomically or physiologically, or perhaps even chemically close to ours," said Carl Sagan. "It would, after all, have had different evolutionary histories in different environments. Nevertheless, our brains and our machines are capable of ultimately understanding each other very well."

The engineers, biologists, physicists, and astronomers who are awaiting the detection of a cosmic radio signal tend to agree with Dr. Sagan. We earthlings have our roots in the universe. So will any other civilization that we may contact. Extraterrestrial life may be life as we know it, or life as we don't know it. It makes little difference. The fact that we share a common galaxy and that we operate under the same physical laws will provide us with some common interests. Some of those interests, perhaps mathematics or science, could provide us with a common language.

SIX

Have They Walked Among Us?

In the mountainous country of Peru, there's a thirty-seven mile strip of land called the Nazca Desert. The region is so isolated that, even today, not many people go there. Nevertheless, well over fifteen hundred years ago, a group of natives constructed a network of roads on this desert. Not only that, they moved pebbles and rocks to form the shapes of monkeys, fish, spiders, and a couple of unidentifiable creatures. The figures are so large they can be seen as a whole only from the air.

Why were these giant figures so carefully laid out? Why would anyone want to build roads that lead from nowhere to nowhere? Some people believe the figures might have been used to guide galactic figures to Earth and that the roads were runways. Could the Nazca Desert once have been used as a landing field for extraterrestrial spacecraft?

Many people claim that extraterrestrial beings have landed upon our planet, not only in Peru, but at various other locations. They say that those alien visitors showed earthlings how to build complex machinery and structures and taught primitive tribes the basics of astronomy and mathematics. There's supposedly a wide range of evidence to support these ideas. Part of it can be found on the walls of caves, where some ancient carvings and paintings appear to some observers to represent spacecraft and helmeted astronauts. Drawings that might be advanced tools and mechanical devices have been found among the ruins of primitive communities.

Two of the best-known pieces of evidence are the Great Pyramid of Egypt and the tall carved figures that dot Easter Island in the South Pacific. Could the ancients have designed and completed such difficult projects? Definitely not, say several widely read authors. The Great Pyramid, stated one man, could not have been built by "puny little men with nothing more than ropes and pulleys. . . . They had to have help."

And that help, according to him, undoubtedly came from outer space.

Other students of ancient civilization don't agree with this viewpoint. They say there's no proof that the ancients couldn't have done these things. Our ancestors were, after all, just as intelligent as we are. It's true they didn't have our years of accumulated knowledge, but one of them could have invented a simple mechanical calculator. An ancient genius who was far ahead of his time could have observed the stars and recognized some simple laws of astronomy.

One writer had little doubt that the Great Pyramid was built by ordinary human beings. "The ancients not only *could* have built such structures," he said. "They *did*. By making it a monument to space, we can ignore the less attractive explanation that it's a monument to a despot, built with years of grinding toil by slaves."

Thor Heyerdahl, who has sailed across the Atlantic and Pacific Oceans in primitive craft, sees no great mystery surrounding the Easter Island figures. He once watched the current inhabitants, using nothing but the simplest of hand tools, carve a new statue and set up an old one that had toppled.

The controversy about extraterrestrial visitations is an ongoing one. There are plenty of people in recent times who claim to have seen alien beings with their own eyes. One such sighting was reported in 1639 by John Winthrop, the first governor of Massachusetts. As he crossed a river in a scow, he saw strange lights in the night sky. They looked like balls of fire that zig-zagged back and forth, darting and zooming "like a pig trying to escape capture."

During World War II, several military pilots were amazed to see unrecognizable objects in the sky. A great number of these unidentified flying objects (UFO's) were reported for the next two decades. Had the earth become a target for extraterrestrial investigation some people wondered. Perhaps our atomic bomb explosions had been seen by residents of another world. Maybe those beings were sending out scouting parties to see if we were planning an invasion of space.

The problem with this idea is time and distance. The nearest star is over four light years from Earth. Thus, the nearest inhabited planet would have to be at least that far away. Suppose there were intelligent beings on that planet. The news of our atomic bomb activity wouldn't have reached them until at least 1950. Traveling at the speed of light, their spacecraft would have taken four or five years to arrive in our solar system in response to the imagined threat. Thus, they wouldn't have been seen near Earth until the mid-1950s, long after the first UFO's had been spotted by World War II pilots.

There are still some UFO reports that remain mysteries, but thousands of them have been identified. Such sightings have turned out to be weather balloons, aircraft, unusual clouds, ball lightning, stars, and dirigibles trailing lighted messages. They have been found to be automobile headlights reflecting off high clouds, a flight of luminescent insects, or an airplane with a high intensity searchlight. A long caravan of cars once chased a suspicious looking bright object across an Arizona desert for several miles. The "alien spacecraft" was later identified as the planet Venus, shining with unusual brilliance in the clear night air.

When scientists investigate a UFO sighting, they talk to the eyewitness and get as many details as they can about the incident. They know, however, that our human senses can be easily fooled. If five people see a traffic accident, the police officer who takes the report is likely to get five different versions of what happened.

College psychology professors often stage mock crimes to show their students how mistaken eyewitnesses can be. Few of the witnesses to the "murder" or "robbery" ever agree on such basic facts as the number of intruders, the clothes they were wearing, the type of weapon, or the exact time of the occurrence.

It's been proven that our eyes and ears aren't one hundred percent reliable under the most ordinary of circumstances. What happens to an astounded farmer when he thinks a galactic spacecraft is hovering over his barn? Or to a terrified motorist when he's on a lonely road and faced with a flying saucer? The human mind tends to "short circuit" when it's asked to absorb such shocking and unexpected visions.

Scientists are also human beings. As such, they must be careful to keep an open mind as they search for the truth behind stories of extraterrestrial visitors. They may or may not believe that aliens have walked among us, but they have to set aside those feelings. Good researchers must resist the temptation to reach for the easiest, most obvious solutions to a mystery. They can't write books using only the evidence that supports what they believe and leaving out all the evidence that doesn't. They have to keep looking at both sides of a question as they search for an answer. They know it may take a long time to find that answer, and there's a possibility they may never find it.

As they're investigating a UFO sighting, scientists must also remember that some people arrange hoaxes for a variety of reasons. Publicity seekers just want to get their pictures in the newspaper, while others like the challenge of seeing whether or not they can "pull it off." Some doctored photographs have made ordinary earthly objects appear to be flying saucers. They have been good enough to fool a few experts in the field of unidentified flying objects.

Until there is solid proof that aliens have landed upon our planet, scientists can only think about, argue about, and discuss the possibility of such visits. Some say since there is no evidence of any visits, there are no intelligent beings out there. Others disagree, saying the "absence of evidence is not evidence of absence." Right now, all we really know is that *we* can't travel through interstellar space. Less than a century has passed since our first airplane flight, and only twenty years since we lifted off into outer space. We're just beginning to explore our own little corner of the universe.

But what about a race of intelligent beings that has hundreds of thousands or even a million years worth of knowledge, compared to our few thousand? Those beings could have found ways to overcome the problems of space travel. They may have discovered new laws of physics and engineering. They could have learned to travel at close to the speed of light, using very efficient and inexpensive energy.

Our own space age is just beginning, but human beings have already lived in semipermanent space stations for more than six months at a time. Is it possible that some very intelligent beings could build a permanent space station upon which thousands of them could live? Such a colony would be completely independent of the home planet. As it journeyed through the Milky Way, it would make no difference that it could travel at only a small percentage of the speed of light. The "galactic nomads" would have no special destination. The space station would be the only home they know.

This idea doesn't seem so strange when we realize that our own planet had been described as a very large spacecraft that orbits the galaxy once every 250 million years.

Space colonies would enable a galactic race to inhabit any solar system, whether or not there was a suitable planet there. Formerly lifeless regions of the galaxy could thus become centers of population. Eventually, one of these colonies could wander into our solar system. Its residents could become our first contact with extraterrestrial life.

It's evident that a combination of science and technology might make it possible for an intelligent race to travel about in the Milky Way. Perhaps some members of such a race have already visited our planet when it was very young. They could have stopped by because of their curiosity, or they may have needed to stock up on some supplies. Some imaginative people believe that the asteroid belt, which encircles the sun beyond the orbit of Mars, is the result of some space travelers' need for minerals. They say that this great ring of space litter is the remnants of galactic mining activity.

Despite such speculations, there's currently no solid proof that aliens ever entered our solar system, let alone landed upon earth. The lack of a "calling card" doesn't mean they were never here. Extraterrestrials could have arrived when life was just beginning to emerge, or when dinosaurs were roaming across the marshes. The most recent alien visit could have occurred ten thousand years ago, which in cosmic terms is only a few seconds. Even at that late date, there would have been no human being capable of taking notes of the event. Any message or unique object left by the visitors could easily have been destroyed by volcanic eruptions, earthquakes, mudslides, or just ordinary everyday weathering or erosion.

Some people say the fact that there are no extraterrestrials walking among us right now is proof enough that they don't exist. But what if you lived in an isolated part of the world? Unless you happened to be looking skyward at just the right moment, you might never see an airplane. The fact that you don't see them doesn't mean they don't exist. If you lived near a busy airport, you'd see dozens of them every day.

In the same way, the scarcity of alien starships

in our sky could mean that the nearest populated planet is so far away that we're not on any regularly traveled cosmic route. It could also mean that an advanced extraterrestrial race might choose *not* to travel through the galaxy.

When considering whether or not aliens are likely to have visited our planet, we should consider the great problems they'd have to overcome to make the trip. It takes a tremendous amount of energy to launch and maintain a spacecraft. Physicist Barney Oliver has calculated that if we were to send a one thousand ton spacecraft on a fifty light-year round trip, the project would consume enough energy to supply the ordinary needs of the United States for three hundred thousand years. For the same amount of energy, we could operate a powerful radio beacon for thirty thousand years. Using that beacon, we could transmit all of our human knowledge and history again and again.

What if we were much more advanced than we are and had discovered a very inexpensive source of energy? Space travel would still be difficult, because there are the problems of time and distance to overcome. If our two Voyager spacecraft were on the right course, it would take them forty to fifty thousand years to reach the nearest star. If they were able to go much faster—at about one tenth the speed of light—it would take only about seventy-five years for the same journey. Even then, the round trip would take two human lifetimes.

As far as we know, the universe has a built-in speed limit. Nothing can go faster than light, but even light takes time to get from one place to another. For instance, when you turn on a switch, it takes a few billionths of a second for a medium-sized room to be lit up. Someone traveling at close to the speed of light would be able to go from here to one of the nearby stars and back again during one lifetime.

There is still another factor to be considered when space travel is being discussed. That factor is "time dilation," which is part of Albert Einstein's theory of relativity. This theory is so complex it's difficult to describe in ordinary language. Einstein used the language of mathematics so it could be more clearly understood.

The principle of time dilation states that the closer the speed of light is approached, the slower time progresses. Imagine a pair of twins, one of whom stays on Earth while the other travels through space at a speed that isn't possible today. The traveler wouldn't realize that anything was happening to him, but all of his bodily processes would be slowing down. The growth of his hair, the beating of his heart, the birth and death of his individual cells, would be proceeding at a slower rate than those of his earthbound twin. Even the hands on his wristwatch would be revolving more slowly. Time would be passing much more quickly for his brother back home.

At ten percent of the speed of light, the difference in the twin's aging process would be slight. At eighty-six percent, the earthbound twin would age twice as fast. If the traveler's speed continues to increase, the difference would become more and more remarkable.

Because of time dilation, a trip covering one hundred light years at close to the speed of light could leave a human being only thirty years older than he was at the start of the journey. From this point of view, time dilation could be a big advantage in space travel. However, if that traveler returned to Earth, he would find that his family and friends had died many years earlier. If the trip were long enough, the earth itself would be so different that he would be a stranger on his own planet. In space travel, much more so than in earthly travel, the saying "You can't go home again," is a painful fact. How many people would be willing to go on such a trip if they knew their farewells would be final?

Most human beings would balk at taking a trip from which there could be no return. Would alien beings feel the same hesitation? Would they decide to stay in their own cosmic neighborhood and develop and improve their own tiny bit of space? If they felt the need to communicate with other planets or space colonies, would they visit them in person? Or would they be likely to use some type of signaling apparatus, such as radio or laser beams? According to Dr. Barney Oliver, perhaps interstellar travel and colonization *don't* exist because interstellar communication *does*.

Has an alien race walked among us? No one can answer that question with certainty at this time. We don't even know if there *is* an alien race, but unless we search for one, we won't have much chance of finding out.

To conduct such an investigation, we don't have to develop a new source of energy, or a different technology. We don't have to figure out how to cope with time dilation.

We don't have to leave our planet and fly billions of miles to walk among *them*. We can stay right here on earth in our own familiar territory, using equipment that's already available for communication. It's possible that another civilization on a distant planet would have made that same decision.

SEVEN

Searching for the Main Street of the Universe

During the past few decades, various people have come up with some imaginative ways of contacting an extraterrestrial civilization. One man sought tirelessly to obtain financing for a giant mirror, so he could reflect sunbeam flashes toward Mars. Another proposed clearing a vast equilateral triangle of Siberian forest, then planting the space with wheat. He hoped that a stellar astronaut would spot the strange patch of vegetation and swoop down to investigate it.

A third man wanted to dig several huge ditches in the middle of the Sahara desert. The excavations were to be five to ten miles long and arranged in geometric patterns. They would be filled with kerosene, which would be ignited on a clear night. His hope was that a group of extraterrestrial beings would spot the blaze and reply with a signal of their own.

Some physicists currently believe that reflected laser beams—a sort of interstellar semaphore—might be the way to send a message to the stars. Others are looking forward to the launching of an interstellar probe.

In June, 1983, eleven years after being launched from Earth, Pioneer 10 became the first man-made object to enter interstellar space. It is carrying a plaque with a drawing of a man and a woman, plus some information about Earth and its inhabitants. Both of the Voyager spacecraft are carrying a "cosmic LP," a two-hour phonograph record. Encoded upon the record are photographs, diagrams, and drawings that represent life on this planet. It also contains greetings from Earth spoken in fifty-three languages, musical selections, sounds of our animal life, the roar of the surf, the cry of a baby, and the soft thump of a human heartbeat.

The LP also contains the words of then United States President, Jimmy Carter. "This is a present from a small distant world, a token of our sounds, our images, our thoughts, and our feelings. . . . This record represents our hopes and our determination, and our good will in a vast and awesome universe."

Thirty-two thousand years will pass before Pioneer 10 draws close to a star. After that approach, a million years will go by before there's another close approach, and still another million years will elapse before the third occurs. Because of the emptiness of interstellar space, the spacecraft's ancient hulk will probably never be seen by alien eyes. In fact, the messages aboard the Pioneers and the Voyagers were composed with little hope that anyone would ever discover them. They were only bottles thrown in a cosmic ocean, a symbol of our deep desire to communicate with a civilization other than our own.

Millions of years from now, those messages will still be journeying through the universe. They may never be found, but they will be a solid piece of evidence that a tiny inhabited planet exists, or once existed, in the suburbs of a small galaxy with the odd name of Milky Way.

Lighting mammoth bonfires in the desert and chopping down Arctic forests aren't effective ways to send greetings to an extraterrestrial race. The use of laser beams for this specific purpose won't be likely for decades. Our cosmic LP has little chance of ever being heard by an alien being. There is, however, one way we could send messages across the vast expanse of space. It could be done by means of a radio transmitter.

The problem is that if we sent the message today, it would have little chance of being heard by an intelligent being until our great-great-great-grandchildren's great-grandchildren were grown. We may be lucky enough to find a "nearby" cosmic neighbor just a few light years away. It's more likely that our message will have to travel a great deal further into the galaxy.

Most scientists feel that we'll be better off listening for a message instead of sending one. There are, after all, stars that are hundreds of millions of years older than our sun. If there are habitable planets orbiting any of those stars, there could have been a highly advanced civilization in existence long before the first human being appeared on earth. What if that civilization had beamed a message into space? The signals could have been sent when we humans were just starting to draw pictures on the walls of caves. They could be out there right now, waiting for us to detect them on one of our radio antennas. If we listen, we'll be able to find out more by picking up just one intelligent signal than we could learn by sending out a hundred of our own.

What's the best way to find this extraterrestrial broadcast? Could it be done by simply continuing the practice of ordinary, everyday astronomy? Perhaps, someday, someone will be studying a pulsar or the birth of a star. That person might suddenly be aware of a different sort of cosmic signal, one that's different from anything found in nature. Further study would bring a gradual awareness that, at last, we've received an intelligent message from somewhere within our galaxy.

The odds against such a fortunate accident ever occurring are overwhelming. Most scientists believe that finding an extraterrestrial message will take an active search by people who are using the most advanced equipment available.

It's generally agreed that SETI should include the examination of medium-sized stars like our own sun. Faint small stars may not give off enough heat to support life. Huge stars have lifetimes of only hundreds of millions of years, a time that is probably too short for life to develop to an advanced stage. Solar type stars, on the other hand, are known to give off just the right amount of energy for life. So far, seven hundred and seventy-three such stars have been identified within a radius of eighty light years from Earth.

The targeted searches of certain stars or groups of stars can best be done by the large, very sensitive radio telescopes, such as the one at Arecibo, in Puerto Rico. These telescopes focus on small areas and can detect very weak signals.

To increase the chances of success, the smaller, less sensitive telescopes can be used for "all sky" searches. With their wide fields of vision, lots of territory can be covered in a few years' time. By carrying on these two types of searches, astronomers make the best use of the limited time they have on the world's busy radio telescopes.

There's much more to the search for an intelligent extraterrestrial signal than just pointing an antenna at a likely location. There are billions of possible "stations," or frequencies over which an alien race might be broadcasting. A group of people could spend several lifetimes trying first one frequency, then another, and another.

Is there a way to narrow down the choices to a smaller group, or "band," of frequencies? Which frequencies would a galactic race be most likely to use?

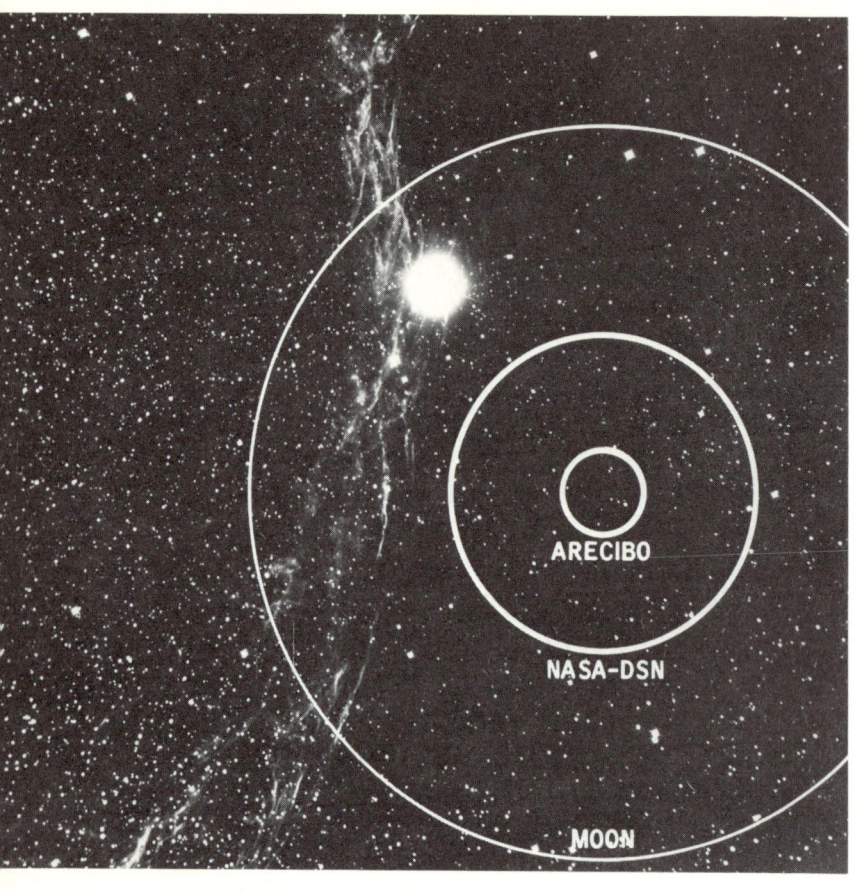

How much of the sky does a radio telescope "see"? If radio telescopes had view finders, like many cameras have, their fields of view would contain many stars. The smaller circles on this photograph represent the fields of view of the large NASA DSN antenna and the 1000-ft Arecibo antenna when they are working near the "water hole" frequencies. For comparison, the largest circle shows the size of the moon.

A faint wispy remnant of an ancient supernova explosion can be seen in this telescopic photograph of a rich field of stars in the constellation Cygnus. The stars are so faint that even the brightest one, the overexposed image near the center of the picture, would just be visible to the unaided eye on a very dark night; none of the others could be seen at all. Hale Observatory photo

All towns and cities have main streets along which people meet to conduct business and exchange news. Does the universe have a main street? Is there a frequency that could provide a common meeting ground for two different races that live trillions of miles apart, two races that may have little in common besides intelligence, an advanced technology, and life itself?

In their attempts to find this band of frequencies, researchers must assume certain things about extraterrestrial beings. First, we believe they'd be as interested in contacting us as we are in contacting them. Second, if they are already sending signals, their technology is at least at our level, and probably far beyond. Such an intelligent group of beings would no doubt be familiar with the workings of the universe, and the laws of physics, chemistry, and astronomy.

They would know that all matter, from the smallest object to the largest, both radiates and absorbs energy. The radiation travels away from the matter at all frequencies and in all directions. Depending upon the temperature of the matter, there's more energy radiated at some frequencies than at others. As an example, when a piece of metal is white hot, most of its energy radiates in the visible, or optical, frequencies. Its heat can be seen as well as felt. As the metal cools, less energy is radiated, and most of it is found as infrared radiation. Since the infrared is invisible to our eyes, the heat can then be felt more easily than it can be seen.

The largest star radiates and absorbs energy. So do the smallest atoms and molecules, but each of these tiny bits of matter radiates and absorbs at a particular frequency instead of all frequencies. When they are packed into a solid object, it's difficult to identify them by their individual "fingerprints." In gases, however, the different atoms and molecules can be easily identified.

An intelligent race would be aware, as we are, that the gaseous clouds in interstellar space are composed of various kinds of atoms and molecules. Galactic scientists would have identified each of them by their characteristic frequencies. These beings would also know that radio transmitters can be tuned to an atomic or molecular frequency. However, since atoms and molecules absorb radiation as well as emit it, any message would be sent close to the frequency, instead of right on it. Otherwise, the travel distance of the message would be limited because it would be absorbed by the gaseous clouds.

Advanced alien beings may assume that astronomers on other planets would have studied interstellar gases to learn about the galaxy, just as we have done. They would probably know that the various frequencies would have caught our attention, and that some frequencies may be better than others for transmitting messages.

The highest and lowest frequencies, which include light rays, ultraviolet rays, and X rays, appear to us to have special problems. Any artificial, or manmade, signals would have to compete with a great amount of natural background emissions from stars and entire galaxies. They would also be weakened when the rays collided with gas and dust and were absorbed.

Another race may have found a way to use the more troublesome frequencies. Nevertheless, at this time, we are better equipped to detect signals from the microwave band of the radio spectrum. Intelligent aliens would surely understand the many advantages that the microwave band has for interstellar communication. It can be used to send signals over long distances with very little interference from natural cosmic noises. It's also very energy efficient, and interstellar gas and dust have very little effect on it. It's likely that an extraterrestrial race would consider the microwave band during its attempts to send messages from a planet far across the galaxy.

These intelligent beings would surely realize that the radio frequency radiation from the hydrogen atom, the most abundant atom in the universe, is located in the quietest part of the microwave band. Would they agree with some of our earthly astronomers that the hydrogen frequency appears to be an ideal candidate for both sending and receiving galactic messages? Could this frequency indeed be the main street of the universe?

Some people with a poetic turn of mind see a special significance in the frequency that carries the "song of hydrogen" from galaxy to galaxy. Under certain conditions, the hydrogen and oxygen of water split into two fragments. One part radiates at a wave-

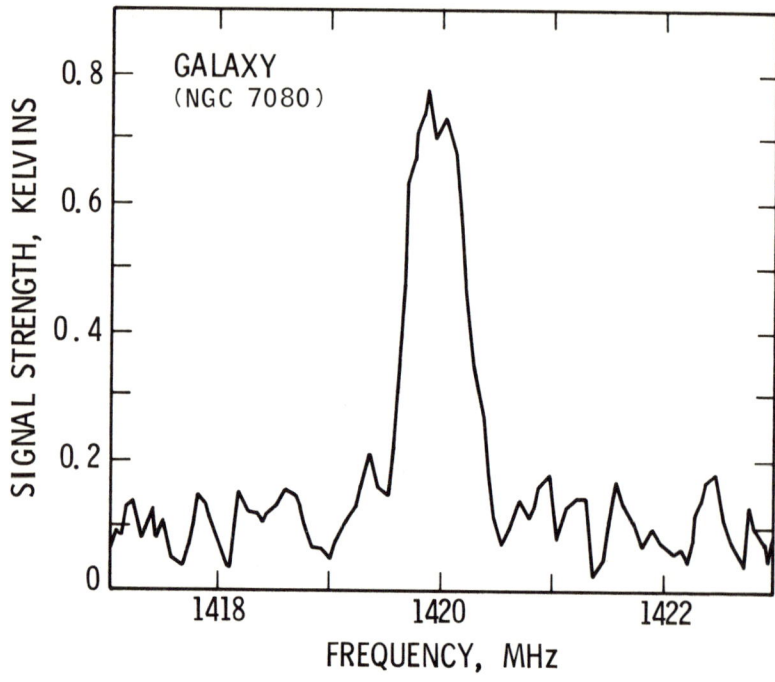

An example of a measurement of the radio emission from hydrogen molecules in a distant galaxy. The giant radio telescope at Arecibo, Puerto Rico was pointed at the galaxy for about a half an hour to build up this spectral signature. Unpublished data courtesy of Peter Wanier

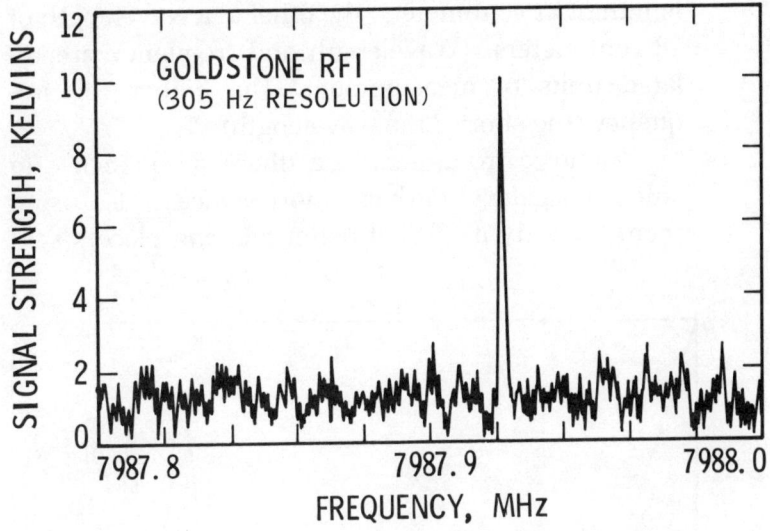

An example of a terrestrial communication signal with narrow bandwidth. It is more than a thousand times sharper than the cosmic hydrogen line (page 72). We can imagine that an extraterrestrial signal might look something like this. Courtesy JPL/Caltech

length of 21 centimeters, the other at a wavelength of 18 centimeters. (Wavelength and frequency are related units of measurement. The higher the frequency, the shorter the wavelength).

Radio astronomers use these frequencies to study our galaxy. Perhaps another race is also using them to study it. "What better meeting place," said

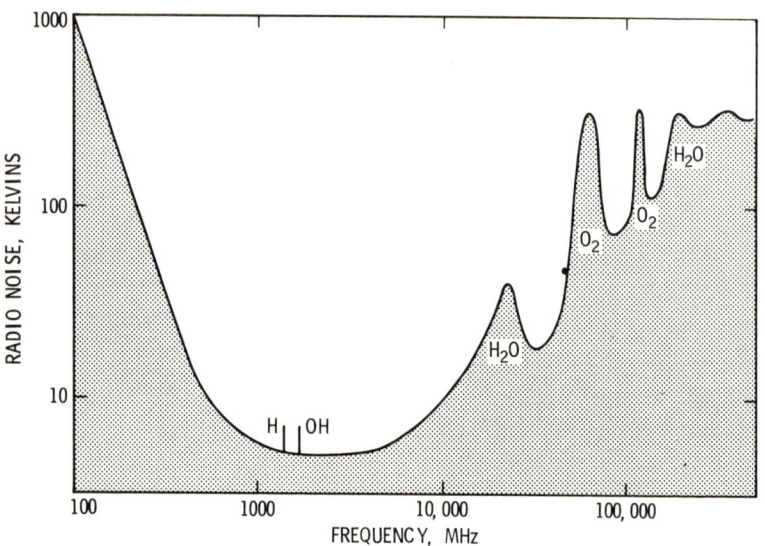

The "Microwave Window" as measured from the earth's surface. Note how the minimum in the cosmic radio noise stretches from about 1000 to 10,000 MHz. Radio noise from our own galaxy rises sharply on the left, while the molecules of water (H_2O) and oxygen (O_2) cloud the radio sky at the higher frequencies toward the right. The symbols for hydrogen (H) and hydroxyl (OH) mark the band of frequencies poetically called the "water hole." Courtesy JPL/Caltech one science writer, "for water-based life to seek its own kind than at the age-old meeting place for all species—the water hole?"

The "water hole" idea is interesting, and it certainly has some scientific merit. Nevertheless, astronomers know they shouldn't rely on only one or even several "magical" frequencies along the spectrum. To increase their chances of success, the search has to include as many frequencies as possible.

But how can any group examine millions upon millions of frequencies? Until recently, the search was agonizingly slow. Computers were bulky, power-hungry, and prone to break down at important moments. Telescope receivers could handle only a limited number of frequencies at the same time. Before a serious search could be conducted, some new technology had to be developed.

As in many scientific projects, engineers and technicians took the first steps toward solving the problems that were standing in the way of the astronomers. In partnership with some physicists, they developed the tiny silicon chip. These "educated grains of sand" are only a small fraction of an inch across, but each one can be etched with thousands of electronic circuits.

The advent of silicon technology made it possible to make computers that are small and durable and that require very little power. Astronomers can also now add specialized electronic computers and signal processors to very sensitive radio receivers. This new equipment enables them to sort through and analyze thousands of frequencies per second. One Harvard University telescope has already begun a four-year, round-the-clock, nonstop sweep of the northern skies. Meanwhile, the National Aeronautics and Space Administration (NASA) is supporting a program to develop instruments by which eight *million* channels of frequencies will be searched each second.

Scientists are hard at work developing strategies for the search. They must answer many questions. Since the cosmic haystack has many dimensions, in which direction should they look? How far away should they look? At which frequencies? What sort of signal would an alien race beam into space? Will it show up on computer screens as a narrow spike, like a single note on a piano? Or will it come on a broad band, like a group of musical chords?

During the search itself, men and women will be watching computer terminal screens and studying computer printout, hoping to find a signal that stands out from the normal cosmic noise. Someday, out of all the static, pops, whistles, buzzes, beeps, and crackles, someone may find that elusive message from a distant civilization. We will have finally met along the main street of the universe.

How does a radio telescope work? What does an astronomer "see" through a radio telescope? The following photos show what one kind of radio telescope looks like and how these instruments are used by scientists and technicians for astronomical research. Courtesy JPL/Caltech

This large microwave antenna, located at Goldstone, California, is operated by the Jet Propulsion Laboratory for NASA. It is used for communication with the many spacecraft that have been launched to explore the solar system and beyond. The antenna can also be used as a radio telescope for scientific studies of the universe, and for searching for evidence of extraterrestrial intelligent life. Courtesy JPL/Caltech

Radio telescopes collect, reflect and focus radio waves in much the same way that optical telescopes are used to amplify visible light. Cosmic radio waves are collected on the saucer-shaped "dish," which measures 210 feet across. The radio waves reflect up to the specially shaped mirrorlike surface at the top of the antenna. From there, the waves are reflected downward and brought to a focus in the "throat" of a "feed horn." Courtesy JPL/Caltech

 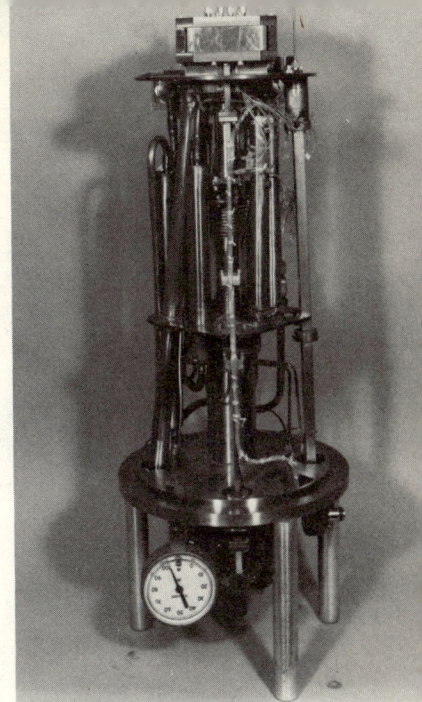

A typical feed horn that is used to collect the focused radio waves. One or more feeds are connected to the input of the "maser," a device that amplifies the incoming radio energy. This unit is pictured on a test rack at the Jet Propulsion Laboratory. Courtesy JPL/Caltech

Stripped of its outer covering, here is a maser amplifier. Its accompanying apparatus consists of electrical connections, a refrigeration unit and a waveguide, which serves as a "pipe" for the incoming radio waves. The maser is cooled to 4 degrees Kelvin, or about 450 degrees below zero Fahrenheit. This low temperature reduces the amount of radio frequency noise generated within the maser and increases its sensitivity to weak cosmic radio signals.

With advancing technology, masers are gradually being replaced by much smaller transistor amplifiers, which are also cooled to achieve greater sensitivity. Courtesy JPL/Caltech

Racks of electronic equipment are needed to control and tune the maser and the microwave receivers that amplify selected frequency bands. Here the radio waves are converted to signals that can be recorded and analysed. This process is similar to an ordinary television set, which acts upon radio waves that have been broadcast from a TV transmitter. The electronics in the TV receiver convert the signal into pictures and sound.

From this console engineers and technicians monitor and control the radio telescope. The racks of electronic equipment control the motors and the hydraulic systems that drive the antenna, keep it properly focused and point it toward the correct direction on the sky.

Chart recorders and video displays must be regularly checked to ensure that the receivers are correctly tuned. As the earth rotates, the antenna position is constantly changing to keep pace with the rising and setting motion of the astronomical objects under study. Temperature and wind can cause subtle errors, which must be corrected to maintain peak performance. Commands and adjustments are entered into the computer, controlling the antenna position to within a thousandth of a degree. Note the TV pictures of the antenna displayed on the monitor on the left of this photograph.

Finally, after the radio waves are collected, reflected, focused, amplified and processed in a computer, astronomers study the results on a video display. The data are usually stored on magnetic tapes or on high-speed computer disks for further processing and study at a later time.

EIGHT

The Rolls of the Cosmic Dice

The universe that lies about is incomprehensibly vast. Yet the conclusion that life exists across this vastness seems inescapable. We cannot yet be sure whether it lies within reach, but in any case, we are part of it all. "We are not alone!"

"It is hard to believe that in all the rolls of the cosmic dice, only one throw has been successful."

"I claim that we are probably the only intelligent species ever to exist in our galaxy. . . ."

"Civilizations light years away might as well not exist. We shall never contact them. We will never find the needle in the cosmic haystack."

"We are alone in space."

These quotes reflect the great range of optimism and pessimism that surrounds the search for extraterrestrial life. Some people believe that it's a waste of time to go on a "fishing expedition," in which our nets are likely to come up empty. Others say that we must continue the search. It may be a gamble, but the stakes are extremely high, and the cost of the "fishing rod" very low. They go on to say that the least that can result from a close examination of promising galactic locations is that we'll add to our fund of knowledge. And if we do find intelligent life, the discovery will be a milestone in the history of humankind.

Is there any way to estimate our chances of success? In an idle moment, Dr. Frank Drake tried to answer that question by writing an equation on the back of an envelope. He meant his "string of educated guesses" to be a mental exercise or a basis for some lively discussions, not as a serious solution to a problem.

To his surprise, "Drake's equation" has been printed and reprinted in books, magazines, and journals. It has sparked controversy and debate. One writer even described it as a "cornerstone in the search for extraterrestrial intelligence." Dr. Drake never thought of his casual scribbling as being that profound.

Drake's equation is written as N equals $R_* f_p n_e f_l f_i f_c L$. The number or value given to each of the seven factors is nothing more than an estimate. When all the factors are multiplied, "N" is intended to be an estimate of the number of advanced technological civilizations in our galaxy. At this point, the value of "N" can be anything from one to hundreds of billions, because no one knows the value of any of the factors. As the gaps in our trail of knowledge are filled with accurate facts, researchers will be better able to supply more accurate numbers.

In the equation, R_* is the rate of star formation in our galaxy.

f_p is the fraction of those stars that develop planetary systems.

n_e is the number of planets that can support life. Presumably, these are earthlike planets.

f_l is the fraction of promising planets upon which life actually occurs.

f_i is the number of inhabited planets upon which intelligent life arises.

f_c is the fraction of planets with intelligent life whose inhabitants learn to communicate with other planets.

L is the average lifetime of a civilization after it develops an advanced technology.

How many stars are formed in the Milky Way each year? Our galaxy is believed to be about ten billion years old. It contains at least 100 billion stars. Thus, every year an average of ten new stars has appeared. However, many more stars were created when the galaxy was young than are being formed now. At this point in galactic history, it's estimated that one new star is born each year.

How many stars are likely to have planetary systems? Astronomers have reason to believe that from one to five percent of all medium-sized solar-type stars have planets orbiting them. This estimate has been based upon the number of stars that have been seen to spin more slowly than others of the same size. The slow spin might be caused by the presence of some planets, or a ring of orbiting material that might develop into planets.

How many of these planets could support life? For the answer to this question, biologists considered our own solar system. They know that earth can support life. Mars is very close to being an earthlike planet. If it had a little more water and were a bit closer to the sun, life might have developed upon it. Perhaps, at one time, it actually did harbor some simple organisms, but so far our space robots haven't found any proof that it did.

Some astronomers have speculated that Jupiter may be supporting some form of living cells. Thus, using the most optimistic figure, it could be said that out of our nine planets, two to three of them could be habitable. However, even if earth were the only one that can support life, it could be said that almost ten percent of all planets are habitable.

On how many habitable planets does life actually arise? Some biologists feel that this number is rather high, because the universe is a factory that produces life's building materials in abundance. In addition, living organisms appeared fairly early in earth's history, and another earthlike planet could undergo the same type of process. Some researchers believe that life would arise on almost every habitable planet. On the pessimistic side, others believe it would arise on only a few.

When living organisms appear, how often do they evolve into intelligent beings? There are wide differences of opinion on this question. One expert on evolution thinks that the chances of intelligent life arising elsewhere are very low, that earth is "appallingly unique."

Many searchers for extraterrestrial life disagree with him. They say that while the exact sequence of events that produced the human race may be unique, the general pathway that leads from primitive cell to intelligent being could be very common.

Because of these contrasting viewpoints, the value put on the factor f_i varies widely. It has been said that intelligent life will eventually appear on any inhabited planet. It's also been said that it will appear on only one out of every trillion inhabited planets.

When intelligent beings evolve, will they develop a technology by which they can communicate with other planetary systems? If they do, will they have a continuing desire to communicate? At this time, most scientists assume that any intelligent race will be a technological race. They also feel that intelligent beings will be curious about the universe. Extraterrestrials will ask questions, search the galaxy, and try to expand their horizons, just as we have done.

Some people have quite different opinions, however. They point out that technology brings not only progress. It also brings problems. Would another intelligent race decide to return to a simpler way of life? Would they slow down, or even reverse, their technological progress? In that case, it's doubtful that they would be sending messages into space.

No one knows what an alien race would do. The estimates of the value of f_c have been set at less than one percent. They've also been set as high as fifty percent.

L, the average lifetime of a technological civilization, may be the most important factor in the equation. During the long history of our galaxy, many millions of intelligent civilizations could have come into existence. After they developed an advanced technology, did they destroy themselves with pollution or nuclear explosions within a few decades or centuries? Or did they find a way to avoid such catastrophes? If technological civilizations tend to die out quickly, there's not much chance that there are many communicating races in our galaxy at any one time.

But what if most technological civilizations don't blow themselves up or poison themselves with pollution? Perhaps they could then last for thousands or even millions of years. In that case, there may be hundreds of thousands of planets and space colonies. Many of them could be beaming messages or launching spacecraft. The chances are good that we'll eventually communicate with at least one of them. At the least, we'll discover its existence.

Perhaps this situation could be better understood by imagining a large, darkened football stadium. At one end, there's a man with his eyes shut. He represents Earth. On the other end of the stadium, stands a woman with a book of matches. Once each hour, at random times, she lights a match and lets it burn for one second. Each lit match represents a single civilization that communicates for a brief time, then stops. Randomly, once each hour "Earth" opens his eyes for a second.

Under these circumstances, there's only one chance in thirty-six hundred that "Earth's" eyes will be open at the same time a match is burning. To see an "alien civilization's" signal, he may have to stay in the stadium for weeks or even months.

On the other hand, what if there were ten thousand "civilizations" flickering on and off at different times? The chances are good one of them would be spotted by "Earth" the first or second time his eyes were opened.

How many "matches" are blinking on and off in the Milky Way? At this time, we don't know, because we've just become able to take our first peek. We can, however, make an estimate based on what we as a human race are doing. Will we continue to pollute our water and air, or will we find ways to keep them pure enough to support life? Will our world leaders find peaceful ways to solve political and economic problems, or will nuclear weapons eventually snuff out our civilization?

Some people believe that the growth of technology is to blame for many of our planet's ills. They say that it causes pollution and enables us to wage a war that could wipe out humankind. Should we stop developing more advanced machines and techniques? If we do, our exploration of the Milky Way will slow down and perhaps stop. If we are inclined to make such a decision, perhaps alien races may do the same. In that case, there would be no point in trying to detect an extraterrestrial signal. There would probably be no beacons sending out messages for our radio telescopes to pick up. Scientists hope the value of "L" is high enough to give us a good chance to make contact with another civilization. They hope we'll eventually learn that intelligently used technology can help us and other societies to improve and extend our lives.

Of what use is the Drake equation? No one, especially Frank Drake, ever said it shows beyond a doubt that a search for extraterrestrial life will end in success. It doesn't even give a good estimate of how large "N" is. All we really know is that "N" is at least one, because we are here. Of all the other factors, only the first three can be given values that are based on known measurements. The rest of the factors have values that range from zero to one to hundreds of billions, depending on the beliefs of the person who's giving the estimate.

Optimism. Pessimism. If. Perhaps. Maybe. On the one hand. On the other hand. Drake's equation hasn't eliminated any of the uncertainty that surrounds the search for extraterrestrial life. If anything, it's added to all the speculating, estimating, wild guesses, and scientific calculations.

If we could send a spacecraft to examine one hundred stars and their solar systems, perhaps we could fill in the values of the factors more accurately.

Until then, Drake's equation remains a fascinating tool, a way to look at the various factors that are involved in the search for alien life. It gives scientists a framework upon which they can hang their arguments or their best guesses. It shows how little we know about our galaxy, and how much work we have to do to fill in the blanks in our store of knowledge.

"We can theorize forever about the possible number of inhabited planets, like the Greek philosophers debating how many teeth are in a horse's mouth," declared one astronomer. "I say it's time to go out and count them."

NINE

Where's My House Key?

Joe was walking home one night when he realized he'd lost his house key. As he searched for it in the light of a street lamp, Bob happened to pass by.

"What's wrong?" Bob asked.

"I lost my house key," Joe replied.

Bob joined in the search. Twenty minutes later, the two friends had looked behind and under every bush, in each clump of grass, and in the gutter. The key was still missing.

"Are you sure you dropped it here?" Bob asked.

"Oh, no," Joe replied. "It actually happened down by the alley. I'm looking for it here because the light is so much better."

If Joe *hadn't* known where he'd dropped the key, his decision would have made a lot more sense. When something is lost, it's natural to start the search in the easiest, most convenient and obvious place. For instance, if your wallet was missing, you'd probably look through all of your pockets or purse, then through your desk, your room, the rest of the house, and the yard. Only after that would you go to the trouble of retracing your steps through the day's activities.

The problem with the search for an extraterrestrial signal is that scientists are looking for something they never had. Nevertheless, they can still avoid making a completely random search. To increase their chances of success, they first decided on the most logical places to detect a signal. Next, because there are several good choices, they picked the ones for which they have the best technology.

At this time, the microwave part of the radio band appears to offer the most advantages. We certainly have the technology to work in this area. Large radio telescopes and highly sensitive receivers are already available, and it doesn't cost much to use them. Radio signals travel at the speed of light. At microwave frequencies about ten to fifty times higher than television frequencies, a transmitter would need only a moderate amount of energy to "shout" above natural cosmic radio noises.

For many reasons, we've already found radio to be a very good way to communicate with each other. We must, however, assume that we are still infants in the realm of technology. As we discover new ways of doing things, we may replace radio with something even better. Perhaps other more advanced beings have already done so. In that case, is there much chance they'd be sending any messages on the radio frequencies?

Many scientists think there is. Why, for instance,

would we send a television signal to some isolated group of people who had never heard of electric lights or automobiles? Such a tribe would have no equipment to receive this kind of message. A flashing light or a drumbeat would be a much better way of getting their attention.

In the same way, a very advanced galactic race probably wouldn't use its newest technology to contact a "backward" civilization such as ours. It would be more likely to use radio, a method of communication that may be used by many races that are just entering their technological age.

Despite this reasoning, radio astronomers may not find an intelligent alien signal in the radio part of the spectrum. If they make a thorough search, a lack of results shouldn't be thought of as a failure. Researchers must expect to run into many dead ends. As time passes, new instruments will enable them to try new types of experiments. No one knows just which experiment will succeed. No one knows which one will give the results that will provide the main link of the trail leading to contact with extraterrestrial life.

There's been a lot of discussion about other likely and not-so-likely places to extend the search for an alien signal. X rays are a possibility, but they must compete with a confusing background of natural cosmic radio noises. Ultraviolet rays are frequently scattered while traveling long distances across space. Even if they get to our solar system, they would be strongly absorbed by the earth's atmosphere. This problem could be partially overcome by the use of orbiting telescopes, but these instruments are very expensive.

Beams of charged particles such as protons and electrons are easily deflected when they enter an interstellar magnetic field, but a very advanced society might have found a way to send signals on them. Our own technology hasn't yet reached a point where we can detect those beams.

Neutron beams have the intensity that's needed to hold a straight course over great distances, but we don't yet have the ability to receive such signals with efficiency. Our equipment isn't sensitive enough, and it's unable to detect the direction of an incoming signal.

During the first part of this century, most scientists and engineers chose to concentrate on radio as a means of communication. They could just as easily have followed a different pathway, one that would have led to the early development of "laser" communication. Lasers are instruments that amplify the intensity of light at the optical, ultraviolet, or infrared frequencies. This amplification creates very intense, very narrow beams of visible radiation, which our eye can see, and infrared radiation, which cannot be seen but can be felt. Laser systems, like radio systems, can be used for both sending and receiving signals.

If we came so close to developing lasers early in our technological growth, perhaps an extraterrestrial race may have taken that route. Maybe that race is sending messages into space on light waves instead of radio waves. We have the equipment to receive those signals, but if they were sent on the optical frequencies, some of them would be absorbed by our atmosphere. Another problem has to do with our current telescopes. They are not able to separate the optical radiation coming from an extraterrestrial laser from the even more intense optical radiation coming from the central star in a distant solar system.

What if a message had been sent on the lower infrared frequencies? If it had, the laser signal would appear very bright in comparison with a star's brightness. This infrared band of frequencies is now being considered for use by the searchers for extraterrestrial life.

Radio. Neutron. Charged particle. Optical. Infrared. These are just a few of the locations of the spectrum from which an alien signal may one day be detected. Right now, our choices are limited, because our technology is limited. Until recently, the situation could be compared to a group of marine biologists who are trying to study the habits of whales. What if they had only a rowboat? Unless a herd of whales just happened to swim close to shore, they wouldn't have much of a chance to do any research. A large, motorized vessel would give them more opportunity to observe the creatures in their natural habitat. But how long would it take them to locate a herd of whales in the vastness of the ocean?

Their chances of success would improve if they

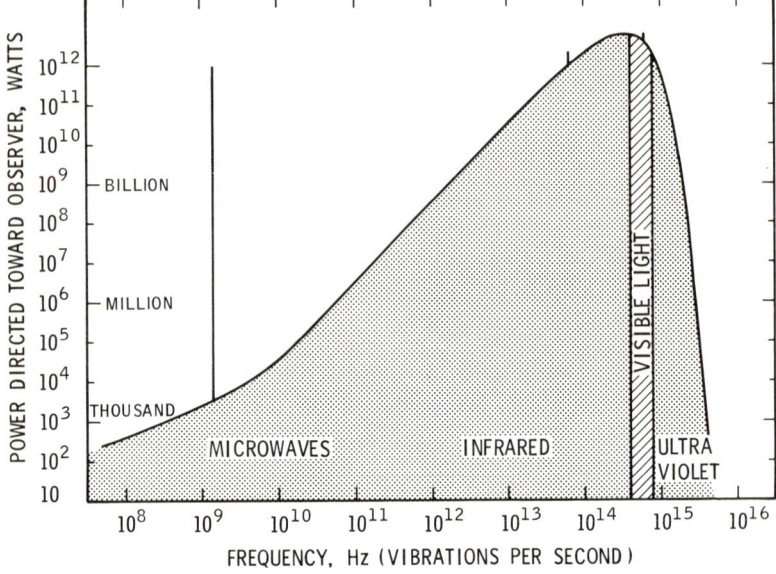

Communication signals compete with the sun. Our sun, and other stars like it, radiate at all wavelengths from the shortest ultraviolet light to the longest radio wavelengths. Here we see how three hypothetical communication signals (the three vertical lines) would contrast with the enormous power of the sun (the shaded region) to an observer near some distant star. Note how the signal in the microwave range stands far above the output from the sun, while signals of identical power transmitted in the infrared and visible are swamped by the sun's light. Such transmissions have not been sent from earth, but we could send them with our current technology if we chose to do so. Courtesy JPL/Caltech

could rent a seaplane, from which they could scan a great area. Now suppose they had detailed up-to-date satellite pictures of the entire ocean. They could immediately discover many groups of whales and see the routes the herds were following. They could do in days what would otherwise take weeks.

The newly developed silicon technology has taken radio astronomers from their "rowboats" and placed them in the "seaplane" stage of their search for extraterrestrial life. By using all the advanced equipment that will soon be available to them, they'll be able to study millions of frequencies a second, and scan a large part of their multidimensional "ocean" at one time. They'll be able to do in minutes what it used to take them years to accomplish.

There are some who say that we should postpone the quest for an extraterrestrial signal until we have expanded our technology. Or until we have more money to spend on it. Or until some of our earthly problems have been solved. They say that the time isn't right to start such a long-term project, one that has no guarantee of success.

One answer to these objections is that we'll have even less chance of success if we wait much longer. Every day our environment is becoming more cluttered with signals from radio, television, defense radars, satellites, and communication links. As each decade passes, increasing numbers of new signals will be competing in the already crowded frequency-space.

We could get around this problem by building

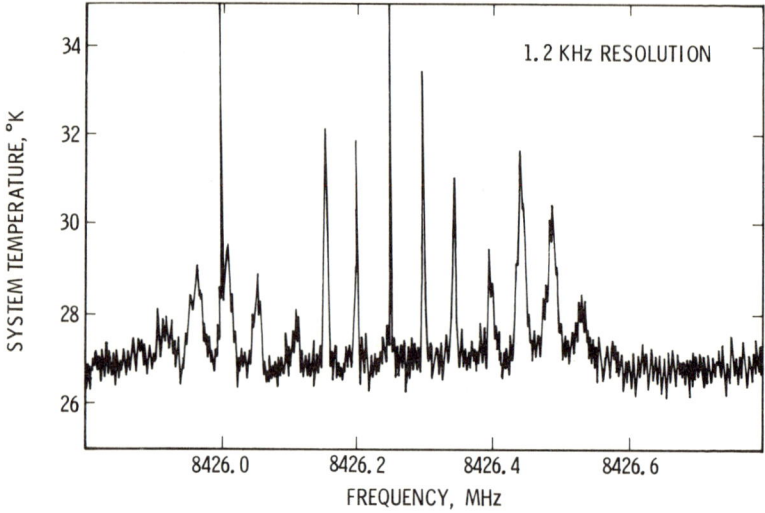

Communication signals are often spread over many frequencies. SETI researchers must learn to sort through this kind of interference as they search for cosmic signals that may be buried in the din of radio noise generated here on Earth and from satellites. Courtesy JPL/Caltech

radio telescopes on the far side of the moon, or upon space platforms, but, the construction and operation of this equipment could add hundreds of millions of dollars each year to the cost of the search. It makes a lot of sense to start now, while the costs are still low.

If the search *is* started now, how long will it take to detect an alien signal? No one really knows, but some say it could happen before the end of this century. Most scientists think that view is too optimistic, that the search will take more time. Everyone agrees, however, that if and when the signal is found, it will be unmistakable. We'll know with certainty that an extraterrestrial civilization has made contact with us, because the signal will be different from any natural noise that's ever reached us from interstellar space.

There's also agreement on another point. The message will probably have come from some alien beings who are ahead of us in their development. Thus, even before that signal is decoded, it may be letting us know that somewhere within our galaxy there's a civilization with a very advanced technology. Those beings may have overcome some technological "growing pains," such as we're having on earth right now. To survive, they may have had to solve problems that their technology created. Were they once threatened with nuclear war, food shortages, and polluted water and air?

If they were, they must have found a way to avert the catastrophe that those problems can cause. That knowledge would give us hope for our own future. It could give us the added courage and determination that we need to survive. It might give us the "push" that we need to rise above our earthly difficulties and take our place in the cosmic family.

TEN

"We Are Made of Starstuff!"

Frank Drake was once a graduate student at Harvard University. One winter day in 1958, he trained the school's radio telescope on the Pleiades star cluster in the constellation Taurus. After several hours of picking up nothing but the usual cosmic crackles and hisses, Drake was getting a little bored. Suddenly he grew alert. There was a strong signal packed into a narrow range of frequency. Natural signals are usually spread out in a broader range of frequency.

Drake wondered if he could possibly have stumbled upon the first intelligent galactic message ever received by a human being. As a test, he pointed the telescope away from the Pleiades to see if the signal would disappear. When it continued, he realized that the supposed intelligent signal was probably nothing but radio noises from an airplane or a passing truck.

What would have happened if that signal *had* been a message from an extraterrestrial civilization? According to Dr. Drake, our little planet might have become a very different place. The certain knowledge that we're not alone in the universe can have a big influence on the way we feel about ourselves and about our place in the cosmic scheme of things. It won't make any difference that the message may have been beamed in our direction fifty or one hundred or even a thousand years ago. The fact that it *was* sent will answer the question we've been asking ever since we turned our eyes toward the stars.

Scientists all around the world will return to their work with a new focus for their enthusiasm. Eventually, they'll have to make a decision. Should we reply to that signal with a message of our own? The reply will take many years to reach our new "pen pals." There isn't going to be any opportunity for idle chit-chat. A serious, involved discussion about sociology, biology, or technology might take generations. In spite of this drawback, one Harvard University professor thinks we should send an answer, then wait for another extraterrestrial signal.

"Imagine," he said, "that a reply to one of our messages was scheduled to be received forty years from now. What a legacy for our grandchildren!"

Our civilization may have to mature for a few more generations before we can transmit a message to the stars. Even then, because of the problems of time and distance and the limit of the speed of light, there's a chance we'll never have a two-way conversation with an alien civilization. We can, however, learn many valuable lessons from any intelligent galactic messages we can detect. Those lessons can be learned by just remaining silent and listening to what extraterrestrials have to say.

Much of our knowledge of the history of the human race has been obtained in the same way—through various forms of one-way communication. How did we learn about the lifestyle of the Egyptians who lived during the reign of the Pharoahs? Certainly not by talking with them on a telephone, or by having them fill out questionnaires. We did it in part by studying the objects they left in their tombs. We learned about the citizens of Pompeii by digging through the layers of ash and dust left by the eruption of Mt. Vesuvius. Our knowledge of Europe in the Middle Ages was gained partially through records kept by monks, not by personal interviews.

Were the years of work that went into the discovery and examination of King Tutankhamen's tomb a waste of time? Would anyone have preferred not to have discovered the ancient cities that were hidden by creeping vines in the South American jungles? Most people agree that the time and effort that went into these projects was worthwhile because of the things we learned. The time we spent searching for extraterrestrial life may lead to even greater knowledge.

One-way communication isn't a fast and easy way to get information. It may take generations to complete an archaeological dig. It may take at least that long to learn whether or not we have any cosmic cousins. In each case, the people who complete the work will have based their discoveries on the work of scores of people who cleared a path ahead of them.

By leaving relics and records beyond them, the ancient earthly civilizations have called to us over a great chasm of time. An extraterrestrial civilization may be calling to us not only over time, but across vast expanses of space. The idea of such a message is exciting to Philip Morrison. "It's a voice not from the past, but from the future," he said. "Archaeology of the future is what it should be called. It's the study of what we're going to become, what we have a chance to become."

Everyone who's involved with the search for extraterrestrial life feels it would be a great loss to all of us if those signals are there and we chose not to look for them.

There are many reasons for continuing the search for extraterrestrial life. It's difficult to put an exact value on some of them. For instance, the search is bound to stretch our minds and our imaginations. It should cause us to be creative and inventive. It should help us to rise above some of our earthly conflicts, or at least put them in the proper perspective.

During the search, we'll be gaining an increased sense of how we fit into the universe as a whole. We humans used to think that our planet was the center of everything that existed. We were proven wrong, but we still held tight to the idea that our sun, at least, was the hub of the universe. Again, we were proven wrong. We used to believe that our solar system and our sun were one of a kind. Now we know that our sun is only one of billions of stars and there are indications that many of those stars may be orbited by planets.

We do not yet have solid evidence, but it now appears that the Milky Way may be a bountiful storehouse, full of everything that's needed for life in its many forms. We know, at least, that interstellar clouds of gas and dust contain life's building materials, and the material that's needed for planetary systems is also there. It's been observed that some basic elements in space have combined to form complex molecules. The first processes that led to life on earth have taken place elsewhere.

All of these pieces of knowledge have led us away from the belief that we're unique or central to anything. We shouldn't stop before we take the final step—to find out whether or not we are one of a kind, or whether we are only one of many species of living beings.

What will happen if, after lengthy search, the evidence appears to indicate that we *are* alone? That knowledge would be just as important as finding out that we're not. It would force us to realize how precious our lives really are. It would give us even more reason to take care of ourselves and our world.

As we search for extraterrestrial life, we'll be expanding our horizons, just as humankind has always done. Our ancestors left their caves to explore wide valleys. When they came to a river, they didn't stop.

They either swam across or built rafts and canoes to get to the other side. As time passed they navigated uncharted seas to find new lands. They kept exploring until they had investigated almost every accessible part of our planet. Now, partly to satisfy our need for adventure, we're turning outward into space to see what is there.

Human beings seem to have a deep desire to respond to challenges. Even to a young child, the words "I dare you" have an almost irresistible ring. Scientists and engineers rose to the challenge of sending men to walk on the moon and of examining the outer reaches of our solar system. Exploring the deepest parts of the ocean was once thought to be an impossible feat. Nevertheless, a few years ago two men in a submersible vessel paid a visit to some of the strange creatures that live seven miles below the surface of the water.

Our next great challenge lies in interstellar space. To turn our backs on that opportunity would be to stifle one of our basic drives. It would be saying that we're satisfied with what we already know; that we're tired of being challenged; that we're not interested in unlocking any more of Nature's secret rooms.

Why should we search for intelligent extraterrestrial life? We should search because we are much more than just specks on a tiny planet revolving around an average sun. We are, instead, an integral part of the universe, made of the same material from which every star, asteroid, and meteor is formed.

Two of the elements from which this material is made were present just a few minutes after the universe was created. Those elements later became gassy clouds of hydrogen and helium, which still later condensed into the first galaxies and into all succeeding galaxies. Stars were born out of this cosmic matter. In the hearts of those stars were forged nearly all the other raw materials that exist today. Billions of years later, when those stars died, that material was recycled into other cosmic bodies.

Many more billions of years passed, and the Milky Way appeared. Our solar system, our earth, and the people upon that earth were formed of matter that had been recycled, perhaps more than once. All of the rocky and metallic substances upon which we're standing today were produced in the shadows of the past, inside innumerable red giants. So were the iron in our blood, the carbon in our genes, and the calcium in our bones and teeth. As Carl Sagan has declared, "We are, indeed, made out of starstuff."

And if there are other beings living elsewhere in our galaxy and in all galaxies, they too are made of starstuff. They are our relatives. Someday when a few more minutes of cosmic time has passed, the atoms in our bodies may become a part of some other solar system, or some other race of beings. Is it possible that, through our own efforts, we can become a part of the cosmic family long before our atoms are blended with their atoms? Can we contact them intellectually before we contact them physically?

Our sun has been in existence for five billion years. Five billion years from now, it will probably die and our solar system will perish. What are we going to do with the time we have left on this planet? Are we going to stay in our own little pocket of space, or are we going to reach out toward the stars? Are we going to try to find our galactic family as we try to find our earthly roots, or are we going to remain alone?

Humankind has used the first part of its life to evolve into thinking beings and to gain some basic knowledge. It could be said that we've completed the first "act" of a cosmic play. Now we've entered an age of technology, the start of the second act. What will we do before the curtain falls? We could continue to be "bit players," with nothing important to say. Or we could take on a major role. We could start by receiving another civilization's message. We could end by sharing our hard-won knowledge with some other young and struggling race of stellar beings.

It's our choice. While we live our lives from day to day and from year to year, we can also focus on events that may occur far in the future. All projects don't have to be completed within one or two decades. We can begin a quest that may go beyond our lifetimes and even our children's lifetimes.

Why should we travel along the trail that may lead to the discovery of extraterrestrial life? When we answer that question, we answer other important questions. The journey involves much more than finding evidence that other intelligent beings exist. SETI involves making discoveries about our own past and our own future. When we've reached our destination, we may discover that we have learned as much about the human race as we have about any alien beings. The search for another civilization may become a search for ourselves.

Glossary

Amino acid one of more than 80 acids that serve as the building blocks of protein.
Ammonia a colorless, gaseous compound of nitrogen and hydrogen. It is lighter than air and has a pungent odor.
Atom the smallest particle of an element that retains the properties that characterize the element. Electrons, protons, and neutrons are components of atoms.
Astronautics the science that deals with the design and construction of space vehicles.
Binary stars companion stars that orbit a common point called their center of gravity. The two stars may be similar or very different in size and brightness.
Black hole A super-dense collapsed body with gravity so strong that nothing, including light, can ever escape.
Carbonaceous chondorite a very rare type of meteorite that is rich in carbon.
Charged particles particles of matter that have positive or negative electrical charge.
Constellation a configuration, or pattern of stars, named for a particular object, person, or animal. Modern astronomers still use constellation names to designate areas of the sky.
Cosmic radio noise the background of radio waves that come from all forms of matter in the universe.
Cosmos the universe thought of as an orderly system.
Density the amount of matter in a given volume. Density equals mass contained in a region of space divided by its volume.

Electron the lightest of the elementary particles that have mass. The electron has negative charge; it shows no evidence of possessing any internal structure.

Enzyme complex organic substances found in living cells. Enzymes are capable of producing special chemical changes in organic materials, as in digestion.

Epsilon Eridani the fifth brightest star located in the constellation Eridanus, the river.

Exobiology extraterrestrial biology, the study of life as it might occur beyond the Earth's environment.

Extraterrestrial originating or existing elsewhere in the universe; not from the earth or its atmosphere.

Factor one of two or more numbers or algebraic expressions that produce a given product when they are multiplied together; the numbers 3 and 4 are factors of 12.

Focus the point where rays of light meet when they are converged by a mirror or a lens.

Frequency the number of vibrations, or cycles, in a given interval of time (usually a second).

Galaxy an enormous collection of stars, which are contained by the gravitational attraction of the group. Typical galaxies contain hundreds of millions to hundreds of billions of stars.

Helium the second lightest and most plentiful element in the universe. Its nucleus consists of two protons and two neutrons.

Hydrogen a tasteless, colorless, odorless, very light gas; the simplest of all atoms. It has just one electron orbiting its nucleus, which is a single proton.

Infrared rays the same electromagnetic phenomenon as visible light but with wavelengths somewhat longer than light and shorter than radio wavelengths.

Intergalactic between galaxies.

Interstellar between the stars.

Interstellar probe a spacecraft designed to travel to other stars and send back information.

Laser a device that amplifies light waves by stimulated emission, which affects the energies of electrons in certain molecules.

Light year the distance traveled by light rays in one Earth year. One light year (1y) equals approximately 6 trillion miles.

Lunar cycle the 29.5-day period over which the phases of the moon pass from new moon through full moon and back to new moon. The time it takes for the moon to orbit the Earth one revolution as measured from the earth-sun line.

Magnetic field the space surrounding a magnetized object within which the magnetic forces can be detected.

Mass a measure of the total amount of material in a body. The gravitational force of a body is proportional to its mass.

MHz the abbreviation for "megaherz," which equals one million cycles per second.

Meteor the luminous phenomenon observed when rocky material from space enters the earth's atmosphere and burns up; popularly called "shooting star."

Meteorite a piece of rocky material from space that has survived its fiery passage through the atmosphere and strikes the ground.

Methane an odorless, flammable gas of carbon and hydrogen.

Microwaves short radio waves with wavelengths an inch or less.

Microwave band the range of radio frequencies with wavelengths from about 100 centimeters (cm) to about 10 cm. The corresponding frequencies range from about 300 Megahertz (MHz) to about 30,000 MHz.

Milky Way Galaxy the galaxy that contains our sun and our system of planets. Our galaxy contains about two billion stars in a spiral formation which, from great distances, would look like a huge pinwheel.

Molecule a combination of two or more atoms bound together; the smallest particle of a chemical substance that has the chemical properties of that substance.

Neutron an uncharged particle of matter, one of the components of an atom. It is 1838 times heavier than the electron.

Neutron star a collapsed, very dense star whose core is composed almost completely of neutrons. Pulsars are rotating neutron stars.

Nitrogen colorless gaseous element found in all known living tissues.

Nucleic acids the genetic material of all life on earth. The two main varieties of nucleic acids are DNA and RNA.

Nucleotide the fundamental building blocks of the nucleic acids.

Organic having to do with living organisms.

Ozone a molecule made of three bound oxygen atoms

Ozone layer a layer of the Earth's atmosphere about 20 to 30 miles above the surface.

Pioneer 10 a US space mission designed to take pictures and measure the environment of Jupiter and Saturn for the first time. The spacecraft, launched in 1972, left the solar system in June 1983.

Proton a positively charged particle, one of the components of an atom. It is 1836 times heavier than the electron. Protons possess three quarks as internal structure, so they are not elementary particles.

Protoplanet a planet in its earliest stage of formation.

Pulsar a rapidly rotating neutron star.

Quark the fundamental components of certain classes of elementary particles, including protons and neutrons. Quarks have a charge of either one-third or two-thirds the charge of an electron.

Quasar a class of astronomical objects that appear starlike, but the energy they emit is several billion times greater than any star. Quasars appear to be the most luminous objects in the universe.

Radio telescope a radio antenna equipped with electronic instruments to make astronomical observations at radio wavelengths.

Radioactive element elements that emit energetic particles, or rays, from the nuclei of their atoms.

Radio astronomy the technique of making astronomical observations at radio wavelengths; a branch of astronomy.

Red giant a large, cool star of high luminosity in the late stage of its stellar lifetime.

Relativity a theory, formulated by Einstein, which asserts that all motion must be defined relative to a frame of reference, and that space and time are relative and not absolute concepts.

Satellite a secondary body revolving around a larger primary body.

SETI the acronym for Search for Extraterrestrial Intelligence, primarily by means of microwave radio exploration (pronounced with short e and i).

Solar eclipse the astronomical event that occurs when the moon cuts off the sun's light as it passes between the earth and the sun. Solar eclipses, either partial or total, are observed somewhere on the earth each year.

Solar system the sun with its planets and their satellites, asteroids, comets and meteoroids. Other stars are believed to have similar systems.

Spectrum a series of radiant energies arranged in order of their wavelengths.

Stellar having to do with stars.

Sunspot a temporary cool region in the sun's radiating atmosphere; it appears dark by contrast against the surrounding hotter regions.

Subatomic particles particles that are much smaller than an atom.

Supernova a cataclysmic explosion of a star. The outer portions of the star are blown into space and the inner core is compressed. A supernova releases more energy in a few days than our sun has radiated in a billion years.

Tau Ceti the name of a star located in the constellation Cetus, the whale.

Time dilation the phenomenon whereby clocks of a moving observer appear to run slow when measured by a stationary observer.

Ultra violet light waves shorter than visible light but longer than X-rays.

Voyager the US space mission consisting of two separate unmanned spacecraft launched in 1977 to explore Jupiter, Saturn and the outer reaches of our solar system.

Water hole a poetic name for the band of radio

frequencies from about 1400 MHz to about 1700 MHz; the band gets its name from two fragments (H and OH) of the water molecule, which radiate at specific frequencies in this band.

White dwarf a collapsed, very dense star whose nuclear fuel is exhausted. The mass of a typical white dwarf is about that of the sun, but its size is about that of the earth.

X-rays light rays with wavelengths ten to one thousand times shorter than visible light.

Bibliography

GENERAL READING

Bracewell, Ronald, *The Galactic Club*. W. W. Norton & Co. Inc., New York, 1979.

Chaisson, Eric, *Cosmic Dawn*. Little, Brown, Boston, 1981.

Edelson, Edward, *Who Goes There?* Doubleday, Garden City, N.Y., 1979.

Ferris, Timothy, *The Red Limit*. Quill, New York, 1983.

Goldsmith, Donald, *The Quest for Extraterrestrial Life*. University Science Books, Mill Valley, CA, 1980.

Jastrow, Robert, *Red Giants and White Dwarfs*. W. W. Norton, New York, 1977.

—*Until the Sun Dies*. W. W. Norton, New York, 1977.

Heidmann, Jean, *Extragalactic Adventure*. Cambridge University Press, London, 1982.

Meeting with the Universe. NASA E.P. 177, U.S. Government Printing Office, Washington D.C., 1981.

Sagan, Carl, *The Cosmic Connection*. Doubleday, New York, 1973.

—*The Dragons of Eden*. Random House, New York, 1977.

Stilley, Frank, *The Search*. G. P. Putnam's Sons, New York, 1977.

Sullivan, Walter, *Black Holes*. Warner Books, New York, 1979.

TECHNICAL PUBLICATIONS

Barrow, J. D. and Silk, J., *The Left Hand of Creation*. Basic Books, New York, 1983.

Cameron, A. G. W., (Editor) *Interstellar Communication*. W. H. Benjamin, 1963.

Goldsmith, D. and Owen T., *The Search for Life in the Universe*. Benjamin/Cummings Publishing, Menlo Park CA, 1980.

Kaufmann, W. J. III, *The Cosmic Frontiers of General Relativity*. Little, Brown & Co., Boston, 1977.

Life in the Universe. NASA Conference Publication 2156, US Government Printing Office, Washington D.C., 1981.

Oliver, B. M. & Billingham, J., *Project Cyclops*. NASA CR 114445, U.S. Government Printing Office, Washington, D.C., 1972.

Sagan, C., (Editor), *Communication with Extraterrestrial Intelligence*. M.I.T. Press, Cambridge, Mass., 1973.

Sagan, C., Article on "Life," *Enclyclopedia Britannica*, Vol. 10, pp. 893–911, 1979.

Search for Extraterrestrial Intelligence. NASA SP 419, U.S. Government Printing Office, Washington, D.C. 1977.

Shklovskii, I. S., and Sagan, C., *Intelligent Life in the Universe*. Holden-Day, New York, 1966.

Sullivan, Walter, *We Are Not Alone*. McGraw Hill, New York, 1964.

Trefil, J. S. and Rood, R. T. *Are We Alone?* Charles Scribner's & Sons, New York, 1981.

Zuckerman, B. and Hart, M. H., *Extraterrestrials, Where Are They?* Pergamon Press, Inc., New York, 1982.

Index

Alexander the Great, 5–6
algae, and beginnings of life on earth, 35
Alpha Centauri, distance, 24
amino acids, and beginnings of life on earth, 34
ammonia, in earth's early atmosphere, 32
Andromeda Galaxy, 13, 22, 24
Arecibo Observatory, Puerto Rico, 1, 67
  radio telescope, fields of view, 68
Aristotle, 5–6
atoms, 28

beams, of charged particles, in carrying extraterrestrial signal, 94
Bell, Jocelyn, 18, 19
Beta Galaxy, 22
Big Bang theory, 27–29
binary star system, 16
black holes, 20–21
Bruno, Giordano, 6

carbonaceous chondrite, 40
Carter, Jimmy, and Pioneer 10 message, 64

civilization, technological, lifetime of, 87–88
Cocconi, Giuseppe, 9
communication, one-way, 102–104
communication signals
  compete with sun, 96
  interference with, 98
computers, and frequency monitoring, 75–76
Copernicus, 6
cosmic egg, 27
cosmic LP, 64, 65
cosmic radio waves, dish for collecting, 78
cosmos, early interpretations of, 2–5
Cygnus, constellation, supernova explosion in, 68
Cyrano de Bergerac, 7–8

dinosaurs, 36–37
dish, for collecting cosmic radio waves, 78
distances, in space, 23–24
Drake, Frank, 1, 9, 83, 89, 101
Drake's equation, 83–84, 89, 90

E.T., film, 43
Earth
　atmosphere formed, 15
　beginnings of life on, 33–36
　first billion years, 32
　second billion years, 32–33
Easter Island, 52, 53
eclipse, solar, early interpretation of, 4
Egypt
　Great Pyramid, 52, 53
　lifestyles at time of pharaohs, 103
electronic equipment, radio telescope, 80
electrons, 28
　in carrying extraterrestrial signal, 94
elements, and living things, 46
energy
　radiation of, 69
　for space travel, 59
Epsilon Eridani, star, 2
exobiology, 44–45
extraterrestrial life
　characteristics, 45–46
　continuing search for, 104–109
　on earth, 58–59
　and exobiology, 44–45
　imaginative concepts, 42–44
　intelligent, 9–10, 47–50, 56–58, 85–87
　listening for messages from, 65–81
　proposed ways of contacting, 63
　proposed ways to attract to earth, 63
　radio in seeking signal from, 92–93
extraterrestrial signal
　agreement about, 99–100
　objections to searching for, 97
extraterrestrial visitations, 52–53

feed horn, for collecting focused radio waves, 78–79
Fontanelle, 8
frequencies, for reaching extraterrestrial life, 67–76

galactic string, 29
Galactic Union Headquarters, 22
galaxies, 25
　formation, 28
　vs. solar system, 23
　spiral, 13
　as storehouse for spare parts needed for life, 40
Galileo, 7, 9
gaseous clouds, in interstellar space, 70
Great Pyramid, Egypt, 52, 53
Green Bank, W.V., Project Ozma meeting, 1–3
guest star, 17, 19

Harvard University, 101
  telescope, 76
helium, 28, 107
Heyerdahl, Thor, 53
human understanding, and search for extraterrestrial life, 105–106
Huygens, Christian, 7
hydrogen, 28, 107
  in earth's early atmosphere, 32
  radio frequency radiation, 71–75

inflationary theory, of formation of universe, 29–30
infrared radiation, energy, 69–70
insects, beginnings, 36
intelligent extraterrestrial life, 9–10, 47–50, 56–58, 85–87
interstellar space
  as next great challenge, 106
  Pioneer 10 in, 64–65
  travel, in science fiction, 22–23
islands, beginnings, 33

Jet Propulsion Laboratory, NASA, 77
Jupiter, 11, 15–16
  likelihood of life on, 85

laser beams, for sending extraterrestrial signal, 64, 65, 94–95
LGM (Little Green Men), 19
life
  characteristics, 45–46
  spontaneous generation theory, 37–38
  in universe, early concept of, 6
  see also extraterrestrial life; life on earth
life on earth
  beginnings, 33–36
  search for master plan, 36–38
light, speed of, 24
light minutes, 24
lightning, and beginnings of life on earth, 33
light seconds, 24
light years, 24–25
Lucretius, 6

maser amplifier, 79
messages, from space, listening for, 65–81
meteorites, ingredients of, 40–41
methane, in earth's early atmosphere, 33
Metrodorus, 5
microbes, and beginnings of life on earth, 35
microwave antenna, 77
microwave band, radio spectrum, 71
microwave window, 74

Milky Way, 17, 24–25, 105, 107
   ingredients for life in, 39–40
   size, 23
Milton, John, 7
molecular colonies, and beginnings of life on earth, 34–35
molecules, 28
moon, early interpretation of, 3
Morrison, Philip, 9, 104

National Aeronautics and Space Administration (NASA), 76
Nazca Desert, Peru, 51
nebula, 12–14, 15
Neptune, 11, 15
neutron, 28
neutron beams, in carrying extraterrestrial signal, 94
neutron star, 18
nucleotides, and beginnings of life on earth, 34

oceanic basins, formed, 32
oceans, and beginnings of life on earth, 34
Oliver, Barney, 59, 61
ozone layer, and beginnings of life on earth, 36

Peru, Nazca Desert, 52
pharaohs, 103

phonograph record, cosmic, carried on Voyager, 64
Pioneer 10, carries information about Earth and its inhabitants, 64
planets
   atmospheres swept away, 15
   birth of, 14
   early interpretations of, 4
   end of life cycle, 17
   habitable, 85
   Jupiter, 11, 15–16
   Saturn, 11, 15, 24
plantlike organisms, and beginnings of life on earth, 35–36
plants, beginnings, 36
Pleiades star cluster, 101
Pope, Alexander, 7
Project Ozma, 9
   Green Bank meeting, 1–3
protons, 28
   in carrying extraterrestrial signal, 94
protoplanets, formed, 14
pulsar, 19–20

quarks, 27, 28
quasars, 12, 25, 29

radiation
   of energy, 69–70
   hot, 28
radio, in seeking extraterrestrial signal, 92–93

Index

radio band, microwave part, in seeking extraterrestrial signal, 92
radio emission, hydrogen molecules in distant galaxy, 72
radio frequency radiation, hydrogen, 71–75
radio noises, originating in space, 12
radio telescope, 12, 77–81
  electronic equipment, 80
  and search for intelligent extraterrestrial life, 9–10
  star search, 67
radio waves, cosmic, dish for collecting, 78
rain
  and early shallow sea, 33
  first to fall on earth, 32
reality, vs. science fiction, 22
replicating molecules, and beginnings of life on earth, 35
Rostand, Edmond, 7, 8

Sagan, Carl, 48, 49, 107
satellites, orbiting, 11–12
Saturn, 11, 15
  distance from Earth, 24
science fiction, interstellar travel in, 22–23
sea, in earth's early years, 33
SETI (search for extraterrestrial intelligence), 9–10, 66, 81, 98, 109

silicon technology
  and frequency monitoring, 75–76
  in seeking extraterrestrial signal, 97
solar stars, listening for messages from, 67
solar system, vs. galaxy, 23
song of hydrogen, 71
space
  distances in, 23–24
  listening for messages from, 65–81
space age, on earth, 57–58
space colonies, 57
spacecraft, 11–12
speed, and space travel, 60–61
spiders, beginnings, 36
stars, 17
  binary system, 16
  birth of, 107
  born each year, 84
  early interpretations of, 3–4
  end of life cycle, 17
  formation, 28
  listening for messages from, 66–67
subatomic particles, 29
sun, 12–14, 15
  as center of universe, 6–7
  communication signals compete with, 96
  distance from Earth, 24
  early interpretation of, 3
  end of life cycle, 16
  origin, 12–14
  "teen-age" years, 15

sun spots, 8
supernova, 26
　explosion, 17–18, 68
survival of the fittest, theory of, 38–39

Tau Ceti, star, 2
Taurus the Bull, constellation, 19, 101
technological civilization, lifetime of, 87–88
telescope
　invented, 9
　to study cosmic bodies, 11–12
temperature, and living things, 45–46
Teng Mu, 6
terrestrial communication signal with narrow bandwidth, 73
thunderstorms, and beginnings of life on earth, 33
tides, and beginnings of life on earth, 34
time dilation, and space travel, 59–62
transistor amplifier, 79
A Trip to the Moon (Rostand), 7
Tsiolkovsky, Konstantin, 8, 9
Tutankhamen, King, 103

UFOs, 53–56
ultraviolet rays
　and beginnings of life on earth, 36
　in seeking extraterrestrial signal, 93
unidentified flying objects (UFOs), 53–56
universe
　Big Bang theory of formation, 27–29
　early concept of life in, 6
　inflationary theory of formation, 29–30
　our relationship to, 26
　understanding how we fit into, 104–105
Uranus, 11, 15

video display, radio telescope, 81
volcanic activity, earth's first billion years, 32
Voyager, 11
　carries cosmic phonograph record, 64

The War of the Worlds (Wells), 42
water hole frequencies, 68, 74–75
Wells, H. G., 42
white dwarf, 16, 20
winds, and beginnings of life on earth, 34
Winthrop, John, 53

X rays
　and black holes, 20–21
　in seeking extraterrestrial signal, 93